Herbert Puchta & Jeff Stranks

G. Gerngross C. Holzmann P. Lewis-Jones

American MORE! 3

Student's Book

CAMBRIDGE
UNIVERSITY PRESS

HELBLING
LANGUAGES

	Grammar	Language Focus and Vocabulary	Skills	MORE!
UNIT 1 Haven't you heard?	• present perfect • irregular past participles • *how long ...?* */for/ since*	• objects **Sounds right** /h/	• ask where people have been • give advice • ask about how long • ask about dreams • read a questionnaire • listen to a conversation • write about your best friend **A Song 4 U** *You've got a friend*	Learn **MORE** through English **That nasty flu!** **Biology**
UNIT 2 Steven Spielberg superstar!	• present perfect + *yet/already* • present perfect with *just* • present perfect vs. simple past	• kinds of movies	• say what you have done • say which movies you like / don't like • talk about movies • read book summaries • listen to the story of a film • write a film review	**Check your progress** Units 1 and 2 Learn **MORE** about culture **The United States** Read **MORE** for pleasure **Casino Royale**
UNIT 3 We're going to use it today	• *will* • *going to* • reflexive pronouns	• geographical features **Sounds right** *going to* stress in compound nouns	• say what you are going to do • talk about preferences • talk about plans/offers • read a short story • listen to a description of an adventure camp • talk about sports activities • write about an adventure camp	Learn **MORE** through English **Glaciers** **Geography**
UNIT 4 Superstitions	• prepositions • common verbs + prepositions • phrasal verbs	• star signs	• talk about superstitions • talk about star signs • find out about people • listen, read, and understand a play • listen and summarize a play • write a review of a story	**Check your progress** Units 3 and 4 Learn **MORE** about culture **Modern books and writers** Read **MORE** for pleasure **Two wishes**
UNIT 5 It's easy, isn't it?	• relative pronouns *who/that* • question tags	• places **Sounds right** intonation in question tags	• ask for information at the movie theater • ask for more information • read a historical text • listen to teenagers talking • write a short letter **A Song 4 U** *Waterloo Sunset*	Learn **MORE** through English **A history of the U.S. capital** **History**
UNIT 6 Teens today	• simple present passive • *make* and *let*	• words for jobs **Sounds right** /ɪ/ vs. /iː/	• talk about ambition • say where things are done • say what people let you do • read and understand a magazine article • listen to the story of an American immigrant • speak about what your parents make and let you do • write about your family	**Check your progress** Units 5 and 6 Learn **MORE** about culture **English around the world** Read **MORE** for pleasure **Burundi boy**

	Grammar	Language Focus and Vocabulary	Skills	MORE!
UNIT 7 I didn't use to like them	• *used to* • *so do I / neither do I*	• music	• talk about what you used to do • agree and disagree • read and match texts and photos • listen to a TV show • speak about performers in a show • write a summary about a pop star or band	Learn **MORE** through English **Musical instruments** **Music**
UNIT 8 Natural disasters	• *too / not … enough* • past passive	• catastrophes **Sounds right** /r/ sound	• express sympathy • explain things in simpler words • talk about when people were born • read and understand a story • listen to the story of an earthquake • speak about things to take to a desert island • write about someone who survived an earthquake	**Check your progress** Units 7 and 8 Learn **MORE** about culture **Manga!** Read **MORE** for pleasure **How to survive earthquakes**
UNIT 9 If I had the money …	• second conditional • *If I were you …* • indefinite pronouns *everyone, someone, no one, anyone*	• computers	• give advice • talk about people • talk about what you would do • ask about how long • read about dilemmas • listen to teenagers talking about dilemmas • complete a questionnaire • write a questionnaire **A Song 4 U** *If I were you*	Learn **MORE** through English **Number challenges** **Math**
UNIT 10 Into the wilderness	• make deductions • causative *have* • infinitives of purpose	• vacations **Sounds right** Question intonation	• give reasons • talk about vacation plans • make deductions • read emails about a trip • listen to an email • write a summary	**Check your progress** Units 9 and 10 Learn **MORE** about culture **Volunteer vacation** Read **MORE** for pleasure **The leopard that lost its spots**
UNIT 11 He told us not to worry	• reported speech 1 • *want/ask/tell* someone to do something	• the environment	• say what you want people to do • read and write about ecology • listen to people talking about their heroes/heroines • talk about your heroes • write a leaflet **A Song 4 U** *We shall overcome*	Learn **MORE** through English **Energy and how to save it** **Science**
UNIT 12 California	• reported speech 2	• physical appearance **Sounds right** Word stress	• justify opinions • identify a person • read a description of Los Angeles • talk about Los Angeles • write about California **A Song 4 U** *California dreaming*	**Check your progress** Units 11 and 12 Learn **MORE** about culture **What a waste!** Read **MORE** for pleasure **The sound of California**

Wordlist

Haven't you heard?

In this unit

You learn
- present perfect
- irregular past participles
- *how long ...? / for / since*
- words for objects

and then you can
- ask about where people have been
- give advice
- ask about how long
- ask about dreams

1 **Read and listen to the dialogue.**

Claire Hi Oliver! I haven't seen you for ages. How are you?

Oliver Great, thanks Claire. How was your summer?

Claire Just great. I had a really good time. We went to Arizona for a week.

Oliver Lucky you! I've always wanted to go there, but I've never had the chance. My parents don't like traveling much.

Claire That's too bad. It's an amazing place.

Oliver Yeah. A lot of people have told me that. Well, maybe I'll go there one day.

Claire Sure you will! Oh, by the way, Oliver, do you have Tom Atkinson's phone number? I want to get in touch with him, and I've lost his number.

Oliver I guess you haven't heard. Tom doesn't live here any more. His family has moved to Michigan. He's been there since last month.

Claire Really? That's a shame. I wanted to show him my photos of Arizona. He's really into photography, and I took some good shots.

Oliver Well, I have his email, so maybe you could send the photos to him that way. Listen Claire, I'm really hungry. Do you want to get something to eat?

Claire Sure! I'm starving! I haven't eaten anything since breakfast. Let's try the new hamburger place on King Street. Have you been there?

Oliver No. So that's two places I've never been! How long has it been open?

Claire About three months, I think. I've heard it's good.

Oliver OK, let's go. You can show me your photos while we eat.

Claire I haven't printed any of the pictures yet, but they're on my camera. I can show them to you.

2 **Write *Claire*, *Oliver*, or *Tom* in each sentence.**

1 .... has been to Arizona.
2 .... has never been to Arizona.
3 .... hasn't heard about Tom.
4 .... has moved to Michigan.
5 .... likes photography a lot.
6 .... has lost a telephone number.
7 .... hasn't eaten since breakfast.
8 .... has never been to the hamburger place.

Get talking Asking where people have been

3 **Listen and repeat.**

Boy 1   Have you ever been to New York?
Girl 1   No, I haven't. Have you?
Boy 1   Yes, I have.

Girl 2   Hi Tom. I haven't seen you since Sunday. Where have you been?
Boy 2   I've been at my grandmother's house for five days!

4 **Ask and answer questions. Use the words on the left and the pictures below.**

Canada
Japan
USA
Mexico
China

A Have you ever been to Canada?
B Yes, I have. / No, I haven't.

A I haven't seen you since yesterday / Monday / this morning. Where have you been?
B I've been sick.

Language Focus

Vocabulary Objects

 Write the number of the correct word in the picture. Then listen and check.

1 sunglasses
2 cell phone
3 CD player
4 MP3 player
5 digital camera
6 palmtop
7 headphones
8 games console

 A

 B

 C

 D

 E

 F

 G

 H

Get talking Giving advice

 Work in pairs. Look at the pictures. Give advice using the expressions below.

A Why don't you ...?
/ You should ...

B OK! Good idea!
/ OK! I will!

1 try it on

2 take a picture

3 use these

4 take it back

5 copy them

6 turn it off

Grammar

Present perfect

1 **Complete the sentences with the verbs on the right. Check against the dialogue on page 4.**

I **have** always [1] .... to go there. (= and I still want to go)
You **haven't** [2] .... (= so you don't know about it)
His family **has** [3] .... to Michigan. (= so he doesn't live here any more)
I **haven't** [4]..................... any of my pictures yet. (= so I can't show you the photographs)

> heard
> printed
> wanted
> moved

We use the present perfect to talk about actions that happened or began in the past (it doesn't matter exactly **when**) and are still relevant **now.** (Read the examples in parentheses above.)
We often use the present perfect with **ever** (in questions) and **never** (in negative statements).
Have you **ever been** there? I **'ve never had** the chance.

2 **Complete the tables with *has / hasn't / have* or *haven't*.**

Affirmative	Negative
I / You / We / They have finished.	I / You / We / They [2]......... finished.
He / She / It [1] .... finished.	He / She / It hasn't finished.

Questions	Short answers
[3]......... I / you / we / they finished?	Yes, I / you / we / they [5]......... / No, I / you / we / they [6].........
[4]......... he / she / it finished?	Yes, he / she / it [7]......... / No, he / she / it [8].........

3 **Complete the sentences with the correct form of the present perfect.**

1   He has ...*worked*....... hard today. (work)
2   My bike is dirty. I .... it. (not wash)
3   .... the game ....? (finish)

4   We .... always .... here. (live)
5   My brother .... never .... a laptop. (want)

Irregular past participles

4 **Complete the table with the appropriate verb.**   gone take run seen had said buy make

be – been	[3]............... – bought	catch – caught	come – come
do – done	eat – eaten	find – found	go – [7]...............
have – [1]...............	know – known	[5]............... – made	[8]............... – run
say – [2]...............	see – [4]...............	[6]............... – taken	think – thought

5 **Complete the sentences.**

1   I'm hungry. I ...*haven't eaten*... anything today. (not eat)
2   He's here now. He's .... out. (be)
3   They aren't here. They .... to the mall. (go)
4   I .... never .... that movie. Is it any good? (see)
5   .... you ever .... of learning Russian? (think)

How long ...? / for / since

6 **Complete with one word in each blank. Check against the dialogue on page 4.**

I haven't seen you [1]..................... ages.
He's been there [2]..................... last month.
How [3]..................... has it been open?

Use *for* to talk about a period of time—**for two hours / for three days / for a year.**
Use *since* to say the exact time when an action or situation began—**since 2005 / since 10 o'clock / since last Friday.**

Use *how long...?* to ask a question about the duration of an action or situation.

7 **Complete with *for* or *since*.**

1 I've had my MP3 player .....since..... Christmas.
2 I've had my palmtop .... six months.
3 My father's worked in that office .... two years.
4 They've lived in that apartment .... 2004.

8 **Write questions using *How long...?* for the answers in Exercise 7.**

We've been students at this school for a very long time!

Get talking Asking about how long

9 **Put the dialogue in the correct order. Listen and check.**

	Roland	About a month. It's great.
☐	**Roland**	About a month. It's great.
☐	**Interviewer**	So, do you use it a lot?
1	**Interviewer**	Hi Roland. Tell me, what's your favorite possession?
☐	**Roland**	Sure, I play games on it and take pictures, and even videos. I've taken a video of my English class. Do you want to see it?
☐	**Interviewer**	How long have you had it?
☐	**Roland**	Hmm, my cell phone, I guess.
☐	**Interviewer**	Maybe another time, thanks!

Get talking Asking about dreams

10 **Match the sentence halves. Then practice them with a partner.**

1 I've wanted to go to Argentina since I was eight years old,

2 I've always wanted to climb a really high mountain,

3 I've always wanted to learn to play the saxophone,

4 I've always wanted to meet a famous person,

5 I've always wanted to sing in a band,

6 I've always wanted to be a writer,

a but I've never climbed a mountain higher than 3,000 meters!

b and I've practiced hard, but no band wants an opera singer.

c but I never have.

d because I saw a movie about tango dancing.

e and now I write instructions for laptops.

f but I've never found the time to take lessons.

Reading

1 Complete the questionnaire.

What kind of friend are you?

1 **Your best friend hasn't called you for two weeks. What do you do?**
- a ☐ You look for a new friend.
- b ☐ You sulk for a while.
- c ☐ You call your friend and try to meet him / her.

2 **You have a problem. Your friend asks you what it is. What do you do?**
- a ☐ You say that you don't want to talk about your problem.
- b ☐ You share your problem with your friend.
- c ☐ You get angry and tell your friend to mind his / her own business.

3 **You have a new haircut, but your friend says you look awful. What do you do?**
- a ☐ You aren't happy, but you know that good friends are honest.
- b ☐ You never talk to your friend again.
- c ☐ You tell your friend that you don't like his / her haircut either.

4 **Your best friend has been sick for three weeks. Last week, you found another friend. Today your best friend is back at school. What do you do?**
- a ☐ You tell your best friend about your new friend.
- b ☐ You don't talk to your new friend any more.
- c ☐ You tell your best friend that you don't have time to meet him / her any more.

5 **You haven't been to the movies since last Christmas. There's a great movie on tonight. You want to go, but your friend wants to go to a party. What do you do?**
- a ☐ Your friend goes to the party, you go to see the movie, and you are still friends.
- b ☐ You don't want to be friends with someone who doesn't like what you like.
- c ☐ You say that you don't really want to see the movie and go along to the party.

Check your score!

Points:
1 a: 1   b: 2   c: 3
2 a: 2   b: 3   c: 1
3 a: 3   b: 1   c: 2
4 a: 3   b: 2   c: 1
5 a: 2   b: 1   c: 3

1–5 points:
It's probably not easy to be friends with you. Try to be a little more understanding! Then you'll make good friends.

6–10 points:
Lots of people would like to be friends with you. You haven't found your best friend yet. Take it easy—you soon will.

11–15 points:
You're an excellent friend, and friendship is really important for you. Other people love being with you.

Look at the words of the song. Put the words in the correct places. Listen and check.

Close
clouds
door
friend
hurt
loud
need
nights

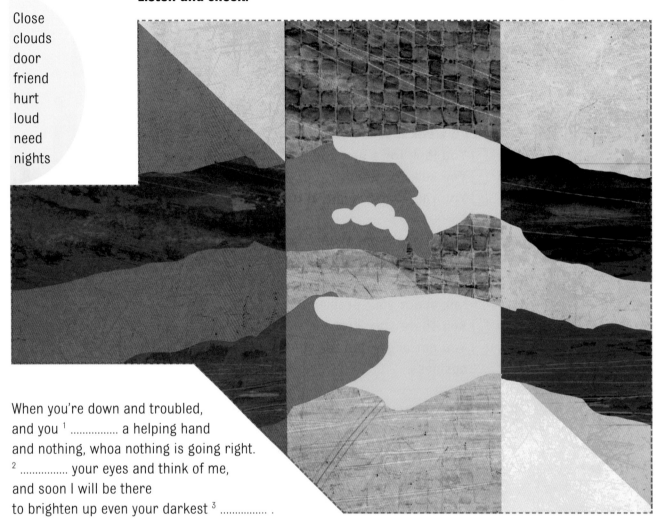

When you're down and troubled,
and you ¹ .... a helping hand
and nothing, whoa nothing is going right.
² .... your eyes and think of me,
and soon I will be there
to brighten up even your darkest ³ ....

You just call out my name, and you know wherever I am,
I'll come running (oh yeah baby) to see you again.
Winter, spring, summer, or fall,
all you got to do is call,
and I'll be there, yeah, yeah, yeah.
You've got a friend.

If the sky above you should turn dark and full of
⁴ .... ,
and that old north wind should begin to blow.
Keep your head together and call my name out
⁵ .... ,
and soon I will be knocking upon your ⁶ ....

Chorus

Hey ain't it good to know that you've got a
⁷ .... ,
people can be so cold?
They'll ⁸ .... you and desert you,
They'll take your soul if you let them.
Oh yeah, but don't you let them.

Chorus

Sounds right /h/

  3 Listen and repeat.

1 Have you heard about Harry?   3 I haven't seen Hank for half a year.
2 He's here and he isn't happy.   4 They stayed at a horrible hotel in Hampton.

Listening and speaking

4 Complete the sentences using the words on the left. Then listen and check. Talk about your best friend.

lies
listens
lends
hear
keeps

1 My best friend always .... me things when I need them. (Sue, 14)
2 Good friends don't just say what you want to .... (James, 14)
3 A good friend .... to your problems. (Les, 15)
4 A good friend always .... a secret for you. (Ken, 15)
5 A good friend never .... to you. (Sharon, 15)

Writing for your Portfolio

5 Read about Joanna's best friend.

My best friend is Natalie. I've known her for six years. We've been friends since our first day of school together. She's really kind and she always helps me if I have a problem. She's really good at math, too. She has helped me with homework many times! We do a lot of things together. We go to the movies and play games. She often stays at my house, and I often stay at hers. We've never had a big argument, only little ones. I think we'll always be friends.

6 Write a short text about your best friend.

That nasty flu!

Key words

temperature	virus	immune system
pain	inhabitants	catastrophic consequences
miserable	sneeze	a flu shot
sickness	cough	medication

1 **Headache, high body temperature, and pain all over the body—when you have influenza, or flu as it is usually called, you feel really miserable. Find out why this sickness can be dangerous and what you can do about it.**

It was November 1918 in Alaska. A ship had just arrived at a nearby harbor. The 80 people in the tiny village of Teller heard about a sickness that the people on the ship had brought with them. But they did not care. They did not often get visitors, and they were very happy to see people from outside their village. They organized a big party for the people on the ship.

The people from Teller did not know that their visitors were carrying a deadly virus. Only a week later, most of the people from Teller became sick. Another week later, 72 out of the 80 inhabitants were dead!

Teller is just one example. In the winter of 1918–1919, this sickness—known as "Spanish flu"—killed more than 50 million people all over the world. Flu comes every year, and most people have had it once. Usually flu is not dangerous, but sometimes it is. In fact, in the twentieth century, there were two more "pandemics." A pandemic is a global outbreak of a sickness with catastrophic consequences. In 1957 the "Asian flu" and in 1968 the "Hong Kong flu" killed a lot of people. In recent years, we have also experienced the "swine flu" pandemic. This flu started after humans were infected by a virus carried by pigs.

INFLUENZA

In many countries doctors recommend high-risk people get a flu shot before the flu season starts. This is what you can do when you already have the flu:

- Stay in bed.
- Drink a lot of liquid such as water and fruit juice.
- Take medicine for fever, aches, and pains.
- Cover each cough and sneeze with a tissue.
- Keep warm.

We hope you're flu-free this year, but if you do get flu, now you know what to do!

2 How does flu spread?

Influenza spreads through a virus. You catch the virus when you breathe in little drops that spray from an infected person when they sneeze, cough, or even laugh. You can also catch flu if the drops get on your hands and you touch your mouth or nose. Influenza viruses are very good at entering a body. They have lots of spikes. They use these spikes to stick to cells and travel through the body.

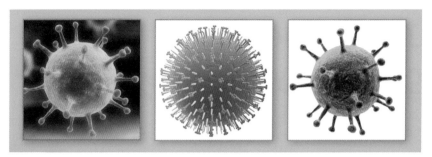

Viruses

When the body's immune system notices the virus, it raises the body's temperature. When body temperature is higher, the virus cannot multiply so easily.

Normally, with the help of medication, it takes the immune system about a week to win the fight against flu. So, why can influenza be so dangerous? This is because young children and older people do not have a very strong immune system. It is also because the influenza virus often changes. Scientists have to develop new medications all the time to fight different flu viruses.

Mini-project Sickness

3 Use a dictionary. Find the names of these sicknesses in your language.

| tuberculosis | chicken pox | food poisoning | malaria |

Choose one of the sicknesses. Search the Internet or check the library to answer the following questions:

1 What causes the sickness? A virus? Something else?
2 Who normally gets the sickness?
3 Is it a dangerous sickness?
4 What can you do when you get it?
5 Have you ever had this sickness yourself?

Flu is a sickness that often occurs during the cold months. It spreads through viruses, and it is especially dangerous for older people and small children. If you have the flu, you have to stay in bed for about a week. You should drink a lot and take medication.
I always get a flu shot before the cold months start. I think it helps.

 Read the magazine article about Steven Spielberg.

Film and theater **NEWS & REVIEWS**

Have you seen the new Spielberg movie yet?

The latest Spielberg movie has just opened, so we thought we'd take a closer look at the man behind the camera.
Laura Davis reports.

People were afraid to go into the ocean after *Jaws*. They wanted to be archeologists after *Raiders of the Lost Ark*. They thought dinosaurs were real after *Jurassic Park*. They cried when they watched *E.T.* and *Schindler's List*. They were shocked by the realities of war in *Saving Private Ryan*. They laughed at *The Terminal* and *Catch Me If You Can*. And they were amazed by the special effects in *War of the Worlds*. They felt this way because of one man, Hollywood's best-known director, producer, and writer: Steven Allan Spielberg.

Spielberg was born in Cincinnati, Ohio, on December 18, 1946. Today he and his movies are famous all over the world. He has already won several Oscars and Golden Globes. He has directed more than 25 movies, and produced more than 50. He hasn't starred in any of his movies yet, but don't be too surprised if you see him on the screen one day.

Has Steven always been so successful? In a word, yes. He made his first amateur movie, an eight-minute western called *The Last Gun*, when he was 12 years old. And he has always been good at making money from movies. When he showed his home movies to other children, he sold tickets, and his sister Annie sold popcorn.

Did you know?

The **producer** controls the preparation of a movie and gets the money for production together.
The **director** is the person who tells the actors how to act in front of the camera.

In this unit

You learn
- present perfect + *yet/already*
- present perfect with *just*
- present perfect vs. simple past
- words for kinds of movies

and then you can
- say what you have done
- say which movies you like/ don't like
- talk about movies

2 Circle T (True) or F (False) for the sentences below.

1 He has won various prizes for his movies. T / F
2 Spielberg only directs movies. T / F
3 When he was 12, he made his first movie. T / F
4 He sold popcorn to the kids who came to see his movie. T / F

Get talking Saying what you have done

 3 Listen and repeat.

A Has Dave seen the new Matt Damon movie yet?
B Yes, he saw it last night.

A Has Dave done his math homework yet?
B No, he hasn't.

4 Work with a partner. Study the table for a minute. Student A asks Student B four questions. Then switch roles.

A Has Dave finished the new Dan Brown book yet?
B Yes, he has. He finished it two hours ago.

finish / new Dan Brown book	(yes) two hours ago
write / an email to Steve	(no)
do / history homework	(no)
buy / *AutoWeek* magazine	(yes) this morning
listen to / new Modest Mouse CD	(no)
finish / the model airplane	(yes) on Monday
see / new Scarlett Johansson movie	(yes) last night
study / for his English test	(yes) last week

5 Think of some recent popular movies, books, computer games, CDs, or magazines and ask your partner if they have seen, read, or heard them.

A Have you seen the new James Bond movie?
B Yes, I saw it on Sunday. It was great!

Language Focus

Vocabulary Kinds of movies

10 **1** Read the article about some of Spielberg's most famous movies.
Write the correct kind of movie under each picture. Then listen and check.

❶

❷

❸

❹

❺

❻

❼

It is difficult to choose a favorite Spielberg movie. There are so many, and he never makes a bad one. Some love his **war** movies, such as *Saving Private Ryan*. Other people go for his **science-fiction** movies, such as *Close Encounters* and *E.T.*

Maybe you prefer his **adventure** movies, like the *Indiana Jones* series, or the **epic** *Schindler's List*. As a producer, Spielberg was responsible for **animated cartoons** such as *Shrek* and even **horror** movies such as *Poltergeist*.

Spielberg has always surprised his audiences with the kinds of movies he makes, and he will surprise us again in the future with something different. After all, his first movie was a **western**!

Get talking Saying which movies you like / don't like

11 **2** Listen and repeat.

A What do you think of adventure movies?
B I think they're exciting.

A What do you think of epic movies?
B I don't really like them. They're always too long.

3 Ask and answer questions about movies with a partner. Use the words and phrases below to help you.

boring   always the same   funny   creative   violent   scary

A What do you think of …?   **B** I think they're …

Grammar

Present perfect + *yet / already*

1 **Look at the text on page 14 and complete the examples below.**

He has [1].................... won several Oscars and Golden Globes.
He hasn't starred in any of his movies [2]....................
Have you seen the new Spielberg movie [3]....................?

You use [4].................... **at the end of questions and negative sentences.**
You use [5].................... **in affirmative sentences.**

2 **Match the sentences to the correct pictures.**

1 She hasn't found the answer yet.
2 The mechanic hasn't fixed her car yet.

3 They haven't called her yet.
4 The tow truck hasn't arrived yet.

3 **Complete the sentences with *yet* or *already*.**

1 Have you seen the new *Spiderman* movie ....?
2 He's .... directed four movies, and he's only 30.
3 We haven't bought our tickets ....
4 I've .... seen this movie twice.
5 They've .... finished filming the new *Superman* movie.
6 Has the new James Bond movie opened ....?

4 **Use the following words to write sentences: *yet* or *already*.**

1 Dana / has / new Keane CD. *Dana already has the new Keane CD.*
2 Nathan / read / the last Dan Brown book ....
3 Dan Brown / not finish / new book. ....
4 Julia / on / a diet. ....
5 John / see / the new Brad Pitt movie. ....
6 Olivia / not see / *The Lion King*. ....

Present perfect with *just*

5   **Put the words in order to create the example sentence. Then check against the text on page 14.**

latest has just The opened. movie Spielberg

We use *just* in affirmative sentences to say that something has happened a short time ago.

6   **Write sentences in the present perfect.**

1   already / movie / start   *The movie has already started.*
2   already / I / be to the movies twice this week
3   just / they / ask for you
4   just / she / hear some great news

Present perfect vs. simple past

7   **Complete the sentences with the present perfect or simple past. Check against the text on page 14.**

He ¹................ (direct) more than 25 movies.
He ²................ (make) his first movie when he was 12 years old.
He ³................ (always be) good at making money from movies.
When he ⁴................ (show) his home movies to other children, he ⁵................ (sell) tickets.

We use the present perfect to talk about an undefined time in the past. When we talk about a specific time, we use the simple past.

8   **Choose the correct form of the verb. Complete the sentences.**

1   I *have found* the money. Here it is! (found / have found)
2   I .... to Chicago for the first time two years ago. (went / have gone)
3   Carmen .... a delicious omelet. Would you like to try it? (made / has made)
4   My parents .... me a new video game last week. (gave / have given)
5   In 2003, my brother .... to New York. (moved / has moved)
6   Claire and I .... friends. We really like each other now. (have become / became)

Get talking   Talking about movies

12

9   **Listen to the interviews and answer the questions.**

1   How many times has Monica seen *Jaws*?
2   How many times has Monica read the book?
3   Why didn't she go swimming when she first saw the movie?
4   Has Dan seen *Jurassic Park*?
5   When did he see *Schindler's List*?
6   Where has Emma seen the *Indiana Jones* movies?

10   **Work in pairs. Talk about movies you have seen. Use the words below to help you.**

A Have you seen any good movies recently?
B I saw…
A What did you like about it?

The actors were
- terrible.
- great.
- good-looking.
- funny.

The story was
- exciting.
- unusual.
- funny.
- real.

The special effects were
- amazing.
- cool.
- excellent.

Reading

1 Steven Spielberg has turned many short stories and novels into movies. Here are some of the books he used. Match the book covers and the descriptions.

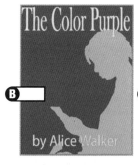
B

C

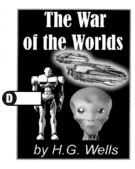
D

E

F

A

1 This is the story of a young black woman named Celie who has to live with a man she doesn't like. However, her female friends help her as much as they can.

2 One day a shark attacks a young lady swimming at night, and the terror begins. A small American town then faces its biggest nightmare. Don't pick this book up before midnight!

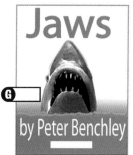
G

3 In this book, a scientist's dream turns into a nightmare when things go very wrong in his theme park on an island in the Pacific Ocean.

4 This is the story of a man who helped thousands of Jews escape the Nazi terror during World War 2.

5 Spielberg filmed the follow-up to the original adventures of three children in Neverland under the title *Hook*.

6 Set in the future, this story is about a police chief whose officers can predict who will commit a crime. One day they predict that he will kill a man he doesn't even know.

7 In this classic science-fiction novel, Martians come to Earth and build huge killing machines. Can the people from Earth fight back?

Reading and listening

 13

2 Listen to Mark talking about his favorite Spielberg movie and number the sentences in the correct order.

1 ☐ A man turns off the electricity.
2 ☐ The visitors escape in a helicopter.
3 ☐ A man builds a dinosaur park.
4 ☐ The children hide from two velociraptors.
5 ☐ Some visitors go to the island.
6 ☐ The dinosaurs escape and kill someone.

3 Listen to the story of *Jurassic Park* again and number the pictures in the correct order.

A

B

C

D

E

F

G

H

Writing for your Portfolio

4 Read the review of *Jurassic Park*. Did the writer like the movie?

I've just seen Jurassic Park. What a great movie. I think it's the best movie Spielberg has ever made. The story is really exciting. It's about some archeologists who find dinosaur blood in a mosquito. A business executive pays some scientists to use it and bring the animals back to life. They are successful and the executive opens a theme park full of real dinosaurs. But before he can open the park to the public, some things start to go horribly wrong.

5 Write a short review of a movie that you have seen recently.

Writing tips: Reviews

- Start your review with your opinion of the movie. Did you like it?
- Add a fact or two. Who directed it? Who are the actors?
- Tell the story. Only give a general idea of what happens. Don't give too many details and don't say what happens at the end!
- When we tell the story of movies, books, and so on, we usually use the simple present tense.

Check your progress Units 1 and 2

1 Complete the names of the objects.

1 palm _ _ _
2 head _ _ _ _ _ _
3 MP3 p _ _ _ _ _
4 sun _ _ _ _ _ _ _
5 digital c _ _ _ _ _
6 cell p_ _ _ _ ☐ 6

2 Complete the titles of the films.

1 w _ _ _ _ _ _
2 s _ _ _ _ _ _ f _ _ _ _ _
3 a _ _ _ _ _ _ _ _
4 w _ _
5 e _ _ _
6 c _ _ _ _ _ _ ☐ 6

3 Complete the dialogues.

A ¹............. you ever .... (be) to
Arizona?
B No, I ² ....

A How long ³.......... he.......... (live) in Michigan?
B He ⁴............ ....(live) in Michigan
⁵ .... four years.

A Have they ⁶......... (see) their new house yet?
B Yes, they ⁷........ already ....(move). I
⁸.......... (go) to see them yesterday! ☐ 8

4 Complete the sentences with the correct form of the present perfect.

1 He ....(not / eat) anything
yet.
2 We .... (know) him for years.
3 She .... (buy) a lot of things.
4 It .... (take) a lot of time.
5 I .... (not find) anything. ☐ 10

5 Write the questions.

1 ....
I think adventure movies are exciting.
2 ....
Good idea! I'll take a picture and give it to
my friend.
3 ....
I've always wanted to be a singer.
4 ....
Yes, he read the new Harry Potter book
last week.
5 ....
No, I haven't done my English homework yet. ☐ 10

6 Complete the text with the correct form of the verb.

I ¹............... never .... (do) anything
wrong, but last year, I ²................ (go)
on a trip with some friends. We ³..............
(stay) at a resort with a lot of stores.
One day, we ⁴..........(decide) to buy some
souvenirs. I ⁵.................... (try) on sunglasses
in one store. It wasn't until I got back to my
hotel that I realized I still ⁶..................... (have)
a pair on my head! I ⁷.............. never ....
(take) anything without paying before.
I ⁸............... (feel) terrible, so I ⁹............. (decide)
to take them back. The next day I did
and things were OK again. ¹⁰............. you
ever .... (make) a mistake like that
before? ☐ 10

TOTAL ☐ 50

My progress so far is ...

☺ great! ☐   😐 good. ☐   ☹ poor. ☐

The United States

1 **How much do you know about the United States? Take our quick quiz and find out.**

1 Which of the following is not in the United States?

a) Alaska   b) New Mexico   c) Ontario

2 Which is the U.S. flag?

3 Which of the following is not a type of coin in U.S. currency?

a) quarter

b) dime

c) pence

4 What is the capital city of the United States?

a) New York, NY

b) Los Angeles, CA

c) Washington, D.C.

5 What is the population of the U.S.?

a) 300 million

b) 500 million

c) 900 million

Do you know?

The United States is the third largest country by land area. It has the biggest economy in the world. It is also one of the most diverse countries in the world. Perhaps the most important document in U.S. history is the Declaration of Independence. It states that all people are equal.

 2 **Listen and decide if the sentences about the Declaration of Independence are true or false.**

1 The Declaration of Independence is an important document.   T / F

2 The Declaration of Independence included a long list of complaints against King George of England.   T / F

3 Delegates signed the Declaration of Independence on July 4, 1776.   T / F

4 Thomas Jefferson wrote the Declaration of Independence.   T / F

MORE! Now you can watch Episode 1 of *The School Magazine!* DVD

Casino Royale

What's the buzz?

Casino Royale, the latest Bond film.

Who's in it?

Daniel Craig is Bond, James Bond. Eva Green stars as Vesper Lynd and Dame Judi Dench is spymaster M.

What's it about?

Daniel Craig is the new James Bond. And the movie makers have decided to make Bond more serious. This time we go back and look at Bond's early days as a spy. Bond is up against super villain Le Chiffre. First he must play him in a game of poker and it's not just about money.

What's the best part?

The chase scene in Madagascar is amazing. Bond gets out of his car to run over walls and up and down cranes. It's completely different from anything you've seen in a Bond movie before.

So is Daniel Craig any good?

Yes, he is. Daniel shows us just how good he's going to be. For the first time you can believe that Bond is a real person, not just some impossible superhero. He's so cool and he's great in the fight scenes.

What's the worst thing about it?

It's not as fun as other Bond movies and that's because this Bond is more serious. There just weren't a lot of laughs.

Hit or Miss?

Hit, definitely. *Casino Royale* keeps old Bond fans happy but has also attracted new fans to the series. Daniel Craig has a bright future playing the world's favorite spy.

But don't just take our word for it:

AMANG! The best one yet! The Aston Martin DBS was such a cool car!
Sophie, 14, Ohio

Easily the best Bond since Connery. Daniel Craig is a terrific new Bond, with better cars and more evil villains. Definitely my favorite Bond.
Alex, 15, Missouri

Wow! I've just seen it on DVD and it was incredible!
Connor, 14, Florida

I thought it was superb! I can't believe all the stunts they have in the movie. I think Daniel is a great Bond!
Rosie, 14, California

I think the movie is great. James' car is so cool!
Peter, 15, Kansas

I think that they could've done better with the car. But overall the movie was good.
Sundeep, 14, Arizona

For **MORE!** Go to www.cambridge.org/elt/americanmore and take a quiz on this text.

In this unit

You learn
- *will*
- *going to*
- reflexive pronouns
- words for geographical features

and then you can
- say what you are going to do
- talk about preferences
- talk about plans/offers

16

1 Read and listen to the dialogue.

Claire	Hi, Rick. What's that?
Rick	My new GPS receiver. You know, Global Positioning System, like the one Dad's got in his car. We're going to use it today. Oliver and I are going to do some geocaching.
Claire	Rick! Listen to yourself! Can you talk to me in English?
Rick	OK, I'll explain it. GPS is a system that tells you how to get to places. It gives you directions.
Claire	Yes, I know.
Rick	Geocaching is like going on a treasure hunt. You need a GPS unit and the coordinates of the place where the treasure is. Then you go hunting, and that's what Oliver and I are going to do. We're really going to enjoy ourselves.
Claire	And what's the treasure?
Rick	Usually it's some small things in a box, a cache. If you find it, you can take something out, but you must put something back in.
Claire	So, you need to take some things with you. What are you going to take?
Rick	I was thinking of your earrings!
Claire	Very funny! So, where's Oliver?
Rick	I don't know. I think I'll call him.
Claire	Maybe he's lost. Why don't you look for him with your GPS?
Rick	Ha-ha. I won't even answer that!

2 **Match the sentence halves.**

1 Rick's dad has a GPS   a is like a treasure hunt.

2 Oliver and Rick are going to   b hasn't arrived yet.

3 Geocaching   c in his car.

4 For everything you take   d putting Claire's earrings into the box.

5 Rick is thinking of   e use the GPS system to find a cache.

6 Oliver   f out, you have to put something back in.

Get talking Saying what you are going to do

17 **3** **Listen and repeat.**

A What are you going to do this afternoon?
B I'm not sure. I think I'll watch a movie.

A Are you going to watch the game tonight?
B No, I can't. I'm going to study for tomorrow's biology test.

4 **Work with a partner. Ask and answer. Use the phrases and ideas below.**

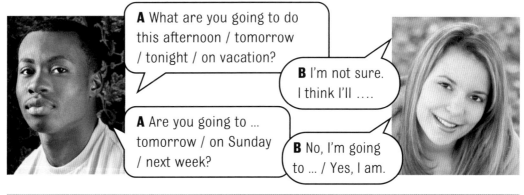

A What are you going to do this afternoon / tomorrow / tonight / on vacation?

B I'm not sure. I think I'll ....

A Are you going to ... tomorrow / on Sunday / next week?

B No, I'm going to ... / Yes, I am.

go swimming   go to the movies   study

go to New York   go to California   play volleyball

Language Focus

Vocabulary Geographical features

18 **1** **Listen. Then write the correct number next to the words on the left.**

- [ ] hill
- [ ] stars
- [ ] valley
- [ ] ocean
- [ ] highway
- [ ] town
- [ ] forest
- [ ] sun
- [ ] fields
- [ ] mountain
- [ ] road
- [ ] village
- [ ] lake
- [ ] river
- [ ] moon
- [ ] beach

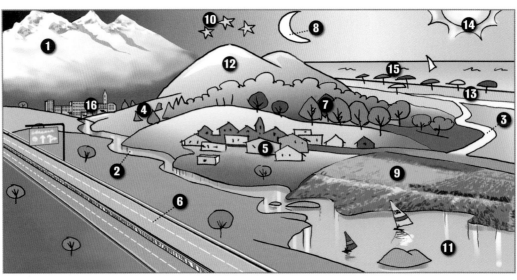

Get talking Talking about preferences

19 **2** **Complete the dialogues using the words on the left. Listen and check.**

road
cache
coordinates
forest
lake
hill

Mark So, where should we go now? Into the ¹............................. ?

Jill No, I'd rather go up the hill. I think the cache is up there.

Mark Are you sure? Read your ²............................. again.

Jill Yes, I'm pretty sure. I don't want to go into the forest. I'd rather walk up the ³......................

Helen Let's take the ⁴............................. down the valley.

Archie I'd rather walk through the field. Then we can go down to the ⁵.............................

Helen No, not the field! I'd prefer to walk on a real road.

Archie But a ⁶............................. is never so close to the road!

3 **Work with a partner. Ask and answer. Switch roles.**

A Would you like to go to the ocean?

B I'd prefer to go to / I'd rather go to ...

Leisure time

go to the movie theater or the gym
play football or play tennis
watch TV or go for a walk

Vacation

ocean or mountains
New York or Florida
the beach or the lake

Grammar

will

> 1 I'**ll** explain it.　　2 I'**ll** help you.　　3 I think I'**ll** call him.

1 **Match the examples with the rules.**

We use *will* to:

a) make offers—.................... ....

b) make decisions (usually at the same time as speaking)—....................

2 **Complete the sentences. Use *will* and the verb in parentheses.**

1 "This problem's very hard." "Don't worry, ..I'll help. you." (help)

2 "Where's Sheila?" "I don't know. .... her." (call)

3 "It's hot in here!" "OK. .... the window if you like." (open)

4 "I'm thirsty." "OK. .... some lemonade." (make)

5 "I don't have enough money for ice cream." "That's OK. .... one for you." (buy)

6 "I don't understand this!" "It's OK, ... it to you." (explain)

going to

3 **Put the words in the correct order. Then check against the dialogue on page 24.**

Rick:　and / I / geocaching. / to / going / are / do / Oliver / some

Claire:　are / What / you / going / to / take?

We use *be going to* to talk and ask about intentions and things we have already decided to do.

4 **Write sentences using the correct form of *be going to* and a verb listed on the right.**

1 My parents' car is very old, so they're going to buy. a new one.

2 When my brother finishes school, he .... a doctor.

3 It's my sister's birthday next week, and I .... her a really nice present.

4 Next Monday is a holiday and we .... our grandparents.

~~buy~~
give
see
be

5 **Circle the correct answer.**

1 **A** Sorry, we don't have any orange juice.

　　B (decides now) OK. *I'll* / *I'm going to* have milk.

2 **A** Is that DVD good?

　　B (decided before) No. *I'll* / *I'm going to* watch
　　a different one.

3 **A** Do you want to go out?

　　B (decided before) No, *I'll* / *I'm going to* finish
　　my homework.

4 **A** I need to look something up on the Internet.

　　B (decides now) OK. *I'll* / *I'm going to* turn
　　the computer on.

Sounds right *going to*

 6 **When we say *going to*, it often sounds like *gonna*. Listen and repeat.**

> I'm going to write you a letter.
> I'm going to put it in the mail.
> And the words in my letter are
> going to make you feel better!

Reflexive pronouns

7 **Look at the dialogue on page 24 and complete the examples.**

Rick! Listen to ....
We're really going to enjoy ....

When the subject and the object of a verb are the same, we use reflexive pronouns as the object.
For example: Stop talking to yourself!

We also use reflexive pronouns if we want to emphasize something about the subject.
For example: She doesn't want any help – **she** wants to do it (**herself**).

8 **Complete with the correct reflexive pronoun.**

Subject pronouns	Reflexive pronouns
I	myself
you	[1] ....
he	himself
she	[2] ....
it	itself
we	[3] ....
you	yourselves
they	themselves

9 **Complete with the correct reflexive pronoun.**

We're going to decorate our room ourselves!

1 We're going to decorate our room
  ourselves.

2 Be careful, Mike! You're going to hurt
  .... !

3 She enjoyed .... at the party.

4 My parents are going to buy ....
  some new clothes.

5 He's a strange person. He always talks to
  ....

6 I'm going to fix dinner .... tonight.

7 My cat washes .... all the time.

8 Bye, Alan! Bye, Susan! I hope you enjoy
  .... tonight!

Get talking Talking about plans/offers

21

10 **Complete the dialogue with the correct phrases. Then listen and check.**

you're going to start
I'm going to hide some things
What are you going to hide there

Marina [1] ....
  .... in our cache near the lake.

Chris Can I come along?

Marina Sure. Does that mean [2] ....
  .... geocaching, too?

Chris I don't think so. [3] ....
  ....anyway?

Marina Oh, a couple of books and a video of
  our last geocaching hunt.

Chris Are people interested in things like
  that?

Marina I hope so!

Reading

 Read the story.

TREASURE HUNT

When Dad said that Kelly and I could go to an adventure camp, I wasn't all that excited. I didn't want to go anywhere with my 12-year-old sister! But I was wrong, and Kelly was actually pretty fun. The best things were the surprise activities—white-water rafting, rock climbing, and a visit to a waterfall. And our guides were really good, especially Ron. He was really cool.

One Friday, Kelly was very excited: "Chris, come quickly, there's a geocaching treasure hunt with Ron tomorrow. But only 20 kids can go!"

"Geocaching?" I thought. I had no idea what it was, but I didn't want to ask her. I'm 14, and she's 12, you know. I asked Ron about geocaching. It sounded great, so Kelly and I signed up.

The next day we started our geocaching hunt. For three hours we looked everywhere—behind every tree, under every stone, in every hole in the ground. Nothing! Then suddenly Kelly shouted, "Here it is!" She had her hand in a hole in the ground, but when she took it out, I knew that it wasn't the "cache" box with a small surprise present in it. My 12-year-old sister had a handful of old coins!

Geocaching treasure hunt!
When: Wednesday 1:00 p.m.
Bring: Good shoes, a snack, and a bottle of water.
Don't forget: One or two small things for the cache!
Write your name on the list.
Only 20 people can go!
See you there! Ron

We showed the coins to Ron and he laughed. "Old coins? Very funny! They're not old. But give them to me." Ron was very nice. He gave me a CD and my sister a candy bar for the coins. Later in the evening, Kelly showed me a coin. "I didn't give him this one," she said. "I wanted to keep it."

Two days later, we went on a trip to a museum near our camp with Ron. We saw many interesting things. Suddenly Kelly shouted, "Look at those coins! They look like my coin!" She had the coin in her hand and it looked exactly like the old coins behind the glass window. One of the security guards heard Kelly. She walked toward us. When Ron saw her, he got very nervous. "Where did you find this coin?" the woman asked. "In the forest," Kelly replied. "We found a lot of them. But we gave them to him!"

Kelly pointed at Ron. Suddenly Ron turned and ran away! The security guard called the police. Two officers came and spoke to us. "These coins are very old," one of them explained. "When you find old coins, you have to give them to the museum. We have to find Ron. He can't keep the coins!"

Two days later the police found Ron. They took the coins away from him. Now they're behind glass in the museum. And next to them there's a little sign. It says:

COINS (A.D. 512)
FOUND BY
KELLY WOODHOUSE

Kelly's very proud of this sign. Well, she is only 12 years old.

2 **Match the sentence halves.**

1 Kelly and her brother, Chris,
2 They really liked the
3 One day they took part in a
4 Chris and his sister didn't find the cache,
5 Ron laughed when the siblings showed Ron.
were
8 The police caught Ron and

a surprise activities.
b but they found some coins.
c him the coins.
d went to an adventure vacation camp.
e very old.
f geocaching hunt with a guide named
6 Two days later, Chris and Kelly went
7 They found out that their coins
g took the coins away from him.
h to a museum.

Listening

22 **3** **Listen to Sarah talking about the adventure camp she went to. Circle T (True) or F (False) for the sentences below.**

1 Sarah went rock climbing and kayaking. T / F
2 It was her first time in a kayak. T / F
3 Her kayak was for one person. T / F
4 Sarah couldn't get out of the water by herself. T / F
5 She hurt herself. T / F
6 She didn't go kayaking again. T / F

Sounds right Stress in compound nouns

23 **4** **When a word is made up of two nouns, we usually stress the first noun more. Listen and repeat. Match the words to make compound nouns.**

rock climbing

rock   riding
class   fall
adventure   work
home   climbing
water   camp
high   room
horseback   way
treasure   hunt

5 **Work with a partner. Make dialogues.**

A What are you going to do this weekend?

B I'm going to go rock climbing.

Speaking

6 Here are six activities you can do at an adventure camp. Number them 1–6: 1 = the activity you think is best, 6 = the activity you think is worst.

☐ canoeing

☐ rock climbing

☐ geocaching

☐ caving

☐ walking

☐ mountain biking

7 Work in groups of three. Discuss three activities for your group to do.

Let's go canoeing.

No, that's boring / too difficult!

I'd prefer to …

Writing for your Portfolio

8 Imagine you are at an adventure camp. Choose some of the activities from Exercise 6 and write a postcard to a friend. Tell him / her:

- if you are enjoying yourself
- what you did yesterday
- what you are going to do for the rest of the camp

MORE fun with Fido

SNIFF! SNIFF! SNIFF!

SNIFF! SNIFF! SNIFF!

SNIFF! SNIFF! SNIFF!

Who needs a GPS with a nose like mine?

Glaciers

Key words

melts	shrinking	sensation	compressed	a large mass of ice
flow	mummy	resources	masses of snow	carved out valleys

24

1 Take this quiz about glaciers. Underline the correct answer. Then listen and check.

1 Glaciers today are getting *smaller / bigger*.

2 We can call glaciers *lakes / rivers* of ice.

3 Very large glaciers can be *40 / 80* kilometers long.

4 Glaciers cover about *2% / 10%* of Earth's land area.

5 Glaciers contain *75% / 25%* of Earth's fresh water.

6 Antarctic ice is about *4,000 / 400* meters thick in some places.

7 Most of the glaciers in the U.S. are in *California / Alaska*.

8 Are there glaciers on every continent? *Yes / No*.

2 Read the text about glaciers.

What are glaciers? Glaciers are masses of snow that have become ice. Sometimes, when snow falls and stays on the ground long enough, it is compressed over many years into a large mass of ice—and that is a glacier.

Glaciers are great rivers of ice. Their own weight makes glaciers flow like very slow rivers. For millions of years, moving glaciers have formed mountains and carved out valleys. They continue to flow and form the landscape in many places.

But today there is a big problem. Glaciers are shrinking fast because the world is getting warmer. This is true in almost every region of the world. An American professor found some plants near a glacier in Peru. Scientists found that the plants were about 5,000 years old. The ice of the glacier covered them for all that time, but when the glacier got smaller, the plants appeared again.

In 1991 hikers found a mummy in the Alps at a height of 3,210 meters. It was a sensation. Scientists discovered that the man crossed the glacier about 5,300 years ago, and snow and ice covered him for thousands of years. But as the weather got warmer and the ice melted, the famous "Iceman" appeared again.

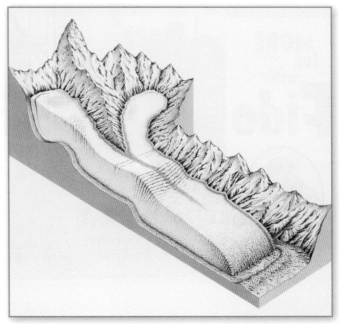

3 **Compare the photos below.**

Pasterze Glacier, 1875   Pasterze Glacier, Today

In many countries, glaciers are major resources for hydroelectric power production. They are also important for watering fields and providing drinking water for cities. But now, as the ice melts, glaciers all over the world will move up the mountains and get smaller.

Perhaps the biggest problem is this: What is going to happen to all the ice on Greenland and in the Antarctic? If the huge masses of ice melt and flow into the ocean, then the level of the water of the ocean will go up, though no one knows how far. As you can imagine, people living on islands only one or two meters above sea level are very worried.

Australian scientists have discovered that the sea level rose about 20 centimeters between 1807 and 2004. Other scientists say that sea levels could rise between 10 centimeters and one meter by the year 2100.

The leaders of Tuvalu, a tiny island country between Hawaii and Australia, have to leave their island in the near future. During the twentieth century, the sea level rose by 20 to 30 centimeters. Scientists say that a rise of up to one meter during this century is possible. As the sea level has risen, the fields on Tuvalu have been flooded by salt water. This means that people do not have fresh water to drink any more, and they cannot water their crops in the fields.

Mini-project Rising sea levels

4 **Check the Internet or your library for facts and ideas about rising sea levels.**

1 Are you superstitious? Read about amazing superstitions from all over the world.

There are many different **SUPERSTITIONS** from all over the world. Here are just a few examples...

CHINA

On New Year's Day, dirt should not be swept out of the house because this will sweep out good luck, too. After January 1, dirt should only be swept out of the back of the house.

THAILAND

Do not tell other people about your bad dream when you are eating. If you do, your dream will come true.

BRAZIL

Many Brazilians believe that you will have money all year if you eat lentils on January 1. So don't forget to eat your lentils at the beginning of the New Year!

KOREA

Some Koreans believe that if you see a magpie in the morning, you'll get good news.

ARGENTINA

Many people in Argentina believe that if you come across money on the sidewalk and pick it up, you'll get even more money. So when you're walking down the street in Argentina, you should be extra careful. There might be people looking at the ground and not at the traffic. Try not to bump into them!

In this unit

You learn
- prepositions
- common verbs + prepositions
- phrasal verbs
- words for star signs

and then you can
- talk about superstitions
- talk about star signs
- find out about people

And what **SUPERSTITIONS** do you believe in?

2 **Complete the statements about superstitions with the correct information from the text.**

1 In China, if you sweep dirt out of the house on New Year's Day ...
2 Some people in Argentina believe they will get rich if ...
3 Some Brazilians believe that if you eat lentils on ...
4 If you want good news in Korea, you must see ...
5 In Thailand, if you tell people about your bad dream while eating, ...

Get talking Talking about superstitions

25 **3** **Listen and repeat.**

A What will happen if I look at the moon at midnight?
B You will meet someone special.

A What will happen if I dream of flying?
B You will go abroad very soon.

4 **Work in pairs. Invent different superstitions. Use the pictures below. Student A chooses three pictures and Student B chooses three sentences. Then switch roles.**

A What will happen if you look at the moon?
B You will find some money.

look at the moon

break a mirror

see two black cats

dream about the sea

find a button

carry an acorn

You will make a new friend.

You will go on a long trip.

You will receive a present.

You will have a bad day.

You will do well on a test.

You will win a lot of money.

Language Focus

Vocabulary Star signs

 ARIES
March 21–April 19

 LEO
July 21–August 22

 SAGITTARIUS
November 22–December 21

 TAURUS
April 20–May 20

 VIRGO
August 23–September 22

 CAPRICORN
December 22–January 19

GEMINI
May 21–June 20

LIBRA
September 23–October 22

AQUARIUS
January 20–February 18

CANCER
June 21–July 20

 SCORPIO
October 23–November 21

 PISCES
February 19–March 20

26 **1** **Some people make up descriptions for star signs for fun. Listen to these descriptions and write the names of the star signs.**

1 A .... is friendly and gets along with other people.

2 .... are happy people. They always smile and laugh a lot.

3 A .... is determined and always gets what they want.

4 A .... is energetic, works hard, and is busy all the time.

5 .... are helpful. They have a lot of friends.

6 .... are intelligent. They love solving all kinds of problems.

7 .... are romantic. They like love stories.

8 .... are dynamic. They love to stay in shape and they play all kinds of sports.

9 .... are passionate. They feel good about the things they do.

10 A .... is flexible and can do more than one thing at the same time.

11 An .... is positive and always sees the good side of life.

12 A .... is a generous person and likes giving presents.

Get talking Talking about star signs

27 **2** **Listen and repeat.**

A What star sign are you?

B I'm a Leo.

A Do you fit the description for a Leo?

B Yes, I do. I have a lot of friends. / No, I don't. I'm …

3 **Work in pairs. Make similar dialogues to those in Exercise 2.**

Grammar

Prepositions

1 Complete the examples with prepositions. Then check against the text on page 34.

... eat lentils [1] .... January 1
... see a magpie [2] .... the morning
... money [3] .... the sidewalk
... dirt should not be swept [4] .... of the house
... your lentils [5] .... the beginning of the New Year
... walking [6] .... the street

2 Look back at the prepositions in the examples. Which ones refer to:

a) time?   b) place?   c) movement?

3 Complete the sentences with the correct preposition.

1 There's a clock .... the wall behind you.
2 Let's meet .... three o'clock ....
   Thursday.
3 I saw him run .... the street and ....
   the bridge.
4 I'm not walking .... that mountain! It's
   too high.
5 The bank is .... to the movie theater,
   across the street from the supermarket.
6 I was born .... the spring, ...
   March 22.
7 He rode his bike .... a curb and fell off.
8 The cat's under the table .... the dining
   room.

Common verbs + prepositions

Some verbs are followed by certain prepositions.

tell someone **about** something
look **at** the ground
What superstitions do you believe **in**?

4 Choose the correct preposition to complete the sentences.

1 Tony! I was just thinking *for/about/in* you.
2 What time do you wake *up/out/into* in the
   morning?
3 Turn *up/through/down* the TV. It's too loud.
4 Come in and sit *down/up/into*.
5 Let me pay *over/in/for* this meal.
6 I'm excited *for/about/in* going on vacation!
7 Do you usually tell him *for/about/on* things?
8 Did you read *for/about/in* the new movie?

5 Complete the sentences with the correct preposition.

| at (x3) | with (x3) | for | on | ~~up~~ |

1 I want you to clean ...up... that mess right now!
2 What do you see when you look .... the
   sky?
3 Turn .... the TV. There's a good movie
   starting.
4 Why are you laughing .... me? What did I
   do?
5 She lives .... Dad, and I live .... Mom.
6 I'm sorry, but I don't agree .... you.
7 I want to apologize .... being rude. I'm
   sorry.
8 He's good .... everything!

Phrasal verbs

6 **Look at the example and answer the question.**

If you *come across* some money on the sidewalk and pick it up...
What does *come across* mean?

a) walk on   b) drop   c) find

Sometimes the meaning of a verb changes completely because of the preposition that follows it. These are known as phrasal verbs.

7 **Circle the phrasal verbs and match them to the correct meaning.**

1 No thanks, I've given up candy. – e
2 The police are looking into the robbery.
3 They've put off their wedding until May.
4 He takes after his father. He really likes sports, too.
5 I bumped into Jim. I haven't seen him for weeks.
6 We made up the dance routine.

a postpone to a later date
b behaves the same as
c meet by chance (not planned)
d create
e stop
f investigate

Get talking Finding out about people

28

8 **Complete the dialogues with the correct phrasal verbs. Then listen and check.**

A I saw Mark yesterday.
B Oh, how is he?
A Great! He ¹.................... soft drinks.
   He looks very healthy!
B Good for him!

A Guess what happened to me this morning?
B You won the lottery.
A No! I ².................... Sally outside the bank.
B Sally! I haven't seen her for ages.

9 **Work in pairs. How well do you know your partner? Complete the sentences.**

1 He/she is interested in ...
2 He/she likes listening to ...
3 He/she is thinking about ...
4 On Sundays he/she gets up at ...

5 He/she enjoys reading about ...
6 He/she likes talking to ...
7 He/she's very good at ...
8 He/she spends a lot of money on ...

10 **Now check with your partner.**

A Are you interested in animals?
B Yes, I am. / No, I'm not.

B Do you like listening to hip-hop music?
A Yes, I do. / No, I don't.

Skills

Listening and reading

1 **Read and listen to scenes 1, 2, and 3 of the play *The Ancient Coin*.**

The Ancient Coin

Mr. Morris

Scene 1

Neil	How long was John in India?
Mrs. Morris	About five years. And do you know what? He brought back an ancient coin.
Neil	A coin? An ancient coin? What for?
Mr. Morris	You can ask him. [*The doorbell rings*] Here he is!

Scene 2

Neil	Why did you bring back an ancient coin from India?
John	Well, if you make a wish and hold the ancient coin in your hand, your wish will come true.
Neil	Wow! How many wishes can you make with it?
John	Three. Here it is. Look at it. You can have the coin. I don't want it any more.
Mrs. Morris	Why not?
John	I'm scared of it. I'm afraid that it will bring me bad luck. Keep the coin Neil, but do not make a wish. I think it might be dangerous.
Neil	OK, don't worry, I won't.

Mrs. Morris

Neil

Scene 3

Neil	Wow. I've got the ancient coin. Now I can make a wish!
Mrs. Morris	No, Neil! Don't!
Neil	Come on, Mom! We have three wishes. If the first wish brings us bad luck, we'll have two more wishes for good luck.
Mrs. Morris	Neil, I don't think you should do this.
Neil	Oh, come on, Mom!
Mr. Morris	Give me the coin. I'll make the wish. Here we go. I wish for a million dollars!

John

2 **Complete the sentences.**

1 John was in India for .... years.
2 He brought a .... from India.
3 If you hold the coin when you make a wish, your wish ....
4 John is scared the coin will bring ....
5 He gives it to ....
6 Neil's father wishes for ....

30 **3** Listen to scenes 4 and 5. Match the sentence halves.

1 Mr. Morris calls Neil and	a it's a police officer.
2 He has won a million dollars	b it's Mr. Morris.
3 Mr. Morris says that he	c Mr. Morris was in an accident.
4 When the doorbell rings,	d will be home in half an hour.
Neil thinks that	e in the lottery.
5 But it isn't Mr. Morris;	f tells him some great news.
6 He tells Mrs. Morris that	

31 **4** Now listen to scene 6. Put the lines into the correct order to write a summary on a piece of paper.

Then Mr. Morris wishes for a million dollars.

3 John gives the ancient coin to Neil.

1 Mrs. Morris tells her family about an ancient coin. Then John Williams arrives. Neil throws the coin into the fire. A doctor calls and tells them that Mr. Morris is fine. Three days later, Mr. Morris calls home and tells Neil that he has won the lottery.

2 He shows them the coin and says, "If you make a wish, the wish will come true." Neil wants to make a wish, but his mom stops him.

A police officer arrives and says that Mr. Morris has been in an accident.

Writing for your Portfolio

5 Read the text about *The Ancient Coin*. What do you agree/disagree with?

The Ancient Coin is a mystery. I love mysteries, so I really wanted to read it. Luckily I wasn't disappointed. I thought it was very good. The beginning was great. The idea of a coin that makes wishes come true is very interesting. I would love to have a coin like that! I wasn't surprised that Mr. Morris wished for money. A lot of people would make the same wish, I'm sure. The best part was when the police officer tells Mrs. Morris about the accident. That put me on the edge of my seat! The only part I didn't like was the ending. I really wanted the family to make another wish.

6 Think of a story you have read or heard recently. Write a short text saying what you thought about it.

Writing tips Giving opinions and supporting them

Before you write, think about the following things:
- Were you interested in the story before you started reading it? Did it disappoint you?
- What were the best parts? Why did you like them?
- Which parts (if any) weren't very good? What was wrong with them?

Remember, every time you give an opinion, write an additional sentence to explain why you feel the way you do.

Check your progress Units 3 and 4

1 Complete the sentences.

1 I climbed to the top of the h _ _ _ .
2 There are bright s _ _ _ _ in the sky.
3 The Beltway is a h _ _ _ _ _ _ around Washington, D.C.
4 The m _ _ _ was shining last night.
5 The f _ _ _ _ was full of flowers.
6 There was a l _ _ _ with a lot of fish. ☐ 6

2 Read the descriptions and complete the sentences.

1 He gets along with other people. He's f _ _ _ _ _ _ _ _ .
2 She likes watching love stories. She's r _ _ _ _ _ _ _ .
3 He likes giving presents. He's g _ _ _ _ _ _ _ .
4 She does a lot and is busy all the time. She's e _ _ _ _ _ _ _ _ .
5 He always gets what he wants. He's very d _ _ _ _ _ _ _ _ _ .
6 She always scores high on exams. She is very i _ _ _ _ _ _ _ _ _ _ . ☐ 6

3 Complete the dialogues. Use *be going to* or *will*.

A What ¹............... he .... (do) tomorrow?
B He's ²............. (see) some friends .
A ³............ you .... (visit) them, too?
B I'm not sure. I think I ⁴............... (decide) tomorrow.

A Which pen would you like?
B I ⁵............ (take) that one, please!

A Amanda and I ⁶................ (have a party) on Saturday.
B ⁷............ Mike .... (come)?
A I don't know. I ⁸......... (call) him tomorrow. ☐ 8

4 Complete the sentences with a reflexive pronoun.

1 They enjoyed .... at the festival.
2 We're going to fix dinner ....
3 Be careful! Don't hurt .... !
4 She decorated the living room .... ☐ 4

5 Complete the sentences with a preposition.

1 He always arrives .... night.
2 They ran .... the road in front of a car.
3 She works .... the morning.
4 We are walking .... the mountain to the top.
5 She takes .... her father. They are very similar.
6 My desk is in front of Sarah's desk. She sits .... me.
7 We're going to leave .... Monday.
8 He walked .... the mall with his friends.
9 She made .... that story. It wasn't true!
10 I'll see him .... dinner. ☐ 10

6 Write the questions.

1 ....
I'd rather go to the ocean than the mountains.
2 ....
On Saturday, I'm going to visit my aunt.
3 ....
I'm a Leo.
4 ....
No, I'm not going to see Mark tomorrow.
5 ....
Yes, I am interested in science. ☐ 10

7 Complete the text with a preposition.

Mark was thinking ¹............... his friend Sarah yesterday. He wanted to apologize ²............ being rude. When she came over to his house last week, she was excited ³............ going on vacation. He laughed ⁴......... Sarah and turned ⁵........... the TV so he didn't have to talk to her. This time he is going to pay ⁶................ a meal for both of them! ☐ 6

TOTAL ☐ 50

My progress so far is ...

☺ great! ☐   😐 good. ☐   ☹ poor. ☐

Modern books and writers

1 Read the extracts from the books and answer the questions. Remember, you don't need to understand all the words in the text.

LEVEL 4 – Kid City

By Andreas Schlüter
Ben told her the rules of his computer game. "Don't you see," he went on. "In the computer game, everyone older than 15 disappears. And that's exactly what's happened here in this city!"
"You mean your computer game has turned real?"
"It may sound crazy, but yes, that's exactly what I mean."
(A) "You're round the twist!"

1 How do you think the two characters feel?
2 Why do they feel like this?

The Blood Stone

By Jamila Gavin
"If this is the house of Geronimo Veroneo, I have a message for you, but let me in for I must speak with you in private. There is danger for all of us."
The voice was foreign, (B) the words used a mixture of Italian and Venetian, so broken and guttural that they could only barely understand him. Carlo listened, (C) frozen by indecision.
Then Teodora's (D) anguished whisper broke through their trance. "Let him in Carlo, let him in."
"No, mother. It could be a trick. We need proof."

1 Do you think the man has come to help them or to hurt them?

2 Read the extracts again and match the underlined sections with the words and phrases below.

1 it was difficult to understand him because he spoke very badly ☐
2 not able to decide what to do ☐
3 frightened and worried ☐
4 You're crazy. ☐

32 **3** Listen to the interview with the author of *The Blood Stone*, Jamila Gavin. Then answer the questions.

1 How old was she when she moved?
2 Why didn't she like school?
3 Where did she work after she left the Guildhall School of Music?
4 Who did she write her books for?
5 What is the location of her new book?

4 **Over 2 U!** Work with a partner and talk about your favorite book. Discuss the title, author, characters, and plot. Say why you like the book.

Do you know?

One of the best-selling children's books in English of all time is *Charlotte's Web*. It's a book about a small spider, a girl, and a pig.

MORE! Now you can watch Episode 2 of *The School Magazine!* DVD

Two wishes

It was the day before the most important test of the year—my math exam. I can't stand math. I just don't understand it. Numbers don't make any sense. Give me words. I love words.

I was looking at my math book on the desk and trying to study. But I just didn't understand it. I kept thinking about my upcoming birthday on Friday. Fail my math exam and good-bye party. I was depressed. My birthday! Then I remembered, don't you get one wish for every birthday? Could I make my wish now, three days early?

I looked at my book and I made a wish. I wished for the best birthday party ever—and then I made a second wish. I wished that for once I could get the best grade in the class. Better than Kate Holmes, better than James Love, better than all those smart kids who always get the best grades.

Then I went to bed. I was tired from all the wishing.

The next day I woke up and went to school. I was nervous. It was exam day and I didn't know anything. I hoped my birthday wish would work. I took my picture of my dog with me and put it on my desk. It's my lucky charm and it always brings me good luck.

Miss Chappell, the math teacher, gave us the exam. I looked at it. Was this math? It looked like Greek to me, all those symbols and strange letters. Luckily, it was multiple choice. I put circles around the A, B, or C and spent the rest of the exam thinking about my party.

The next day I got to school I was really nervous. Was this the end of my party? We got to the classroom, but Miss Chappell was not there. The principal arrived. Miss C was home sick. We would find out our grades on Monday. I was free!

The party was great. Everyone was there. Kate Holmes and James Love talked about the math exam all night. I didn't care. I just danced.

So did my wish really come true? I had the best party ever, that's true. Well, remember that I said you get one wish every birthday? Well, I made two. And the second wish? Well on Monday morning Miss C was there. I got my grade—a big fat "F." The worst in the class. Yes, it was that bad!

Read the story again and put the following events in the correct order.

- ☐ She had a great time at the party.
- ☐ She took her exam.
- ☐ She failed the math exam.
- ☐ She went to bed.
- ☐ She made a birthday wish.
- ☐ She got her grade.
- ☐ [1] Jenny was trying to study.
- ☐ Her teacher was sick.

For **MORE!** Go to www.cambridge.org/elt/americanmore and take a quiz on this text.

In this unit

You learn

- relative pronouns *who/that*
- question tags
- words for places

and then you can

- ask for information at the movie theater
- ask for more information

33

1 **Read and listen to the dialogue.**

Claire This homework on Washington, D.C., isn't easy, is it? Question 8: "What's the name of the building that is 88 meters high?" It's the Washington Monument, isn't it?

Karen No, you're wrong. The Washington Monument is 169 meters tall.

Claire How do you know that?

Karen I did some Internet research before you came over. I think the answer is the U.S. Capitol. OK, next question. "What's the name of the institute that includes 19 museums?" I know that. It's the Smithsonian.

Claire The only question I can answer is the one about the person who lives in the White House! That's the president!

Karen Thankfully, we have the Internet to help us.

Claire Mr. Collins wants this tomorrow, doesn't he?

Karen Yeah. So come on, let's finish it. Rick'll be here any minute to pick us up.

(A few minutes later)

Rick Hi. Are you ready to go? Have you finished the assignment about Washington, D.C.?

Claire Yes, we have. I bet you haven't finished it, have you?

Rick No, I haven't had time.

Karen It's harder than you might think! We'll wait for you to finish before we go to the movies.

Claire But after that you'll have to buy us ice cream!

2 **Circle T (True) or F (False) for the sentences below.**

1 Claire thinks the assignment is difficult. T / F
2 The U.S. Capitol is the tallest building in Washington, D.C. T / F
3 The Smithsonian includes 19 museums. T / F
4 Their teacher wants the answers to the assignment the next day. T / F
5 Rick hasn't finished the assignment about Washington, D.C. T / F

Get talking Asking for information at the movie theater

34 **3** **Listen and repeat.**

Girl	Excuse me, what movie is showing on Screen 10?
Clerk	*Spiderman.* Would you like a ticket?
Boy	Excuse me, the main movie hasn't started yet, has it?
Clerk	No, they're still showing the previews.
Girl	Do you still have tickets for the new Spielberg movie?
Clerk	No, sorry! That sold out hours ago.

35 **4** **Match the questions and answers. Then listen and check.**

Questions
1 Do you still have tickets for the 9:00 show?
2 How much is a ticket?
3 What kind of movie is *Eternal Sunshine*?
4 Can we sit anywhere?
5 How long is the movie?

Answers
a It's a comedy, but some parts are sad.
b Let me see. It's about 89 minutes.
c Yes, we have a lot left.
d It's $4, please.
e Of course, we don't have reserved seating here.

5 **Work in pairs. Practice the dialogues from Exercise 4.**

Language Focus

Vocabulary Places

36 **1** Listen and write the words under the pictures.

stadium
park
exhibition
museum
superstore
farmer's market
auditorium
movie theater
aquarium
concert

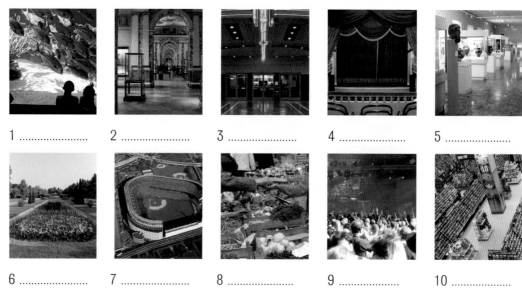

1 .... 2 .... 3 .... 4 .... 5 ....

6 .... 7 .... 8 .... 9 .... 10 ....

Get talking Asking for more information

37 **2** Complete the dialogues with the sentences. Listen and check. Act them out.

Yes, it is. I think it's open from 12 to 6.   How much are they?
We don't do discounts.   I'm pretty sure, but we can call them.
Yes, we have. How many do you want?

At the auditorium box office

Natasha   Excuse me, do you have any tickets left for tonight's performance?
Assistant   ¹ ....
Natasha   Two please.
Assistant   OK. I have two tickets in the second row.
Natasha   ² ....
Assistant $10 each.
Natasha   Is there a discount for students?
Assistant   I'm sorry. ³ ....
Natasha   Alright. I'll take them anyway.

Fred   Is the record store open on Sundays?
Ken   ⁴ ....
Fred   Are you sure? I don't want to go there and find it's closed.
Ken   ⁵ ....

3 Work with a partner. Pick a place/an event from Exercise 1 and make up a
dialogue. Ask about opening times, tickets, prices, and discounts.

Grammar

Relative pronouns *who / that*

1 **Complete the examples. Then check against the dialogue on page 44.**

What's the name of the building [1] .... is 88 meters high?
What's the name of the institute [2] .... includes 19 museums?
The president is the person [3] .... lives in the White House.

We use the relative pronouns *who /that* to talk about people.
We use the relative pronoun *that* to talk about animals and things.

2 **Circle the correct word.**

1 I have a friend *who / that* hates pizza!
2 That's the restaurant *who / that* has the best food in town!
3 An atlas is a book *who / that* has information about different countries.
4 I like people *who / that* give me presents.
5 Alison's the girl *who / that* always gets the best grades in our class.
6 I never buy clothes *who / that* are expensive.

3 **Complete the definitions.**

1 A nurse is a person *who helps take care of sick people.*
2 A map is a thing
   ....
3 A magnifying glass is a thing
   ....
4 A sheepdog is an animal
   ....
5 A traffic officer is a person
   ....

4 **Make one sentence from two.**

1 A programmer is a person. He / She writes programs for computers.
   A programmer is a person who / that writes programs for computers.
2 A dictionary is a book. It tells you the meanings of words.
   ....
   ....
3 A pilot is a person. He / She flies planes.
   ....
   ....
4 A superstore is a very large store. It sells almost everything.
   ....
   ....
5 Ferraris are Italian cars. They are very expensive.
   ....
   ....

Question tags

5 **Look at the dialogue on page 44 and complete the examples.**

1 This homework on Washington, D.C., isn't easy, ... ?
2 The answer's the Washington Monument, ... ?

With positive statements we usually use a negative question tag.
With negative statements, we usually use a positive question tag.
Question tags are commonly used to confirm information or invite the listener to agree.

6 **Complete the sentences using the question tags below.**

aren't you	does she	wasn't it	didn't we	won't you	doesn't she

1 You aren't Canadian, *are you* ?   5 You're going to be at the party, ... ?
2 It was cold there, ... ?   6 We enjoyed ourselves, ... ?
3 You'll help me, ... ?   7 Your sister doesn't like me, ... ?
4 She speaks English, ... ?

7 **Complete the sentences using the question tags below.**

does she	didn't you	has he	aren't they	will it

1 He hasn't gone, ... ?   4 You went to Tokyo last year, ... ?
2 She doesn't live in Chicago, ... ?   5 It won't happen, ... ?
3 They are Chinese, ... ?

Sounds right Intonation in question tags

8 **When we are sure about something, our intonation goes down at the end. When we are unsure, our intonation goes up at the end. Listen and repeat the sentences then circle (U) for unsure and (S) for sure.**

1 It's cold today, isn't it? U / S   4 I'm not late, am I? U / S
2 You don't like me, do you? U / S   5 You didn't forget, did you? U / S
3 They're nice people, aren't they? U / S   6 It isn't wrong, is it? U / S

Skills

Reading

1 **Read the text.**

The Great Fire Chicago

The great Chicago fire is one of the most famous fires in history. The fire started on the evening of October 8, 1871. It had been a very dry summer in the months leading up to the fire. And Chicago had many wooden buildings.

The fire killed 300 people and destroyed more than 17,000 buildings in just 27 hours.

The cause of the fire remains a mystery to this day, but the popular legend is that it was started in Mrs. O'Leary's barn. Mrs. O'Leary was milking a cow when the cow kicked her lamp. The barn was set on fire and spread quickly.

These were some of the eyewitness accounts of what people saw:

"We could see across the river at the cross streets that where yesterday was a populous city was now a mass of smoking ruins. All the way round we encountered thousands of people; but the excitement had given way to a terrible grief and desolation." - Alexander Frear

"The immense piles of lumber on the south of us were all afire…. Dense clouds of smoke and cinder rolled over and enveloped us, and it seemed almost impossible to breathe." - Lambert Tree

"There was a strip of fire between two and three miles long, and a mile wide, hurried along by a wind, sweeping through the business part of this city…. It was a grand sight, and yet an awful one." - William Gallagher

After the fire, people stopped using wood to build structures in Chicago.

2 **Circle T (True) or F (False) for the sentences below.**

1 In 1871, Chicago had a very dry summer. T / F

2 It is believed that the fire began in a church. T / F

3 Many buildings in Chicago were made from wood. T / F

4 The fire killed 300 people. T / F

5 The fire went on for weeks. T / F

6 Only about 1,000 buildings were damaged. T / F

7 After the fire, people no longer built structures in Chicago from wood. T / F

8 The fire started in the mid-afternoon. T / F

Listening

3 **Listen to three teenagers. Write what they like about New York City under their names.**

music
the subway
food from all over
 the world

 James

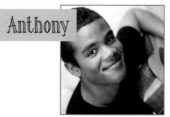 Anthony

 Julie

....

40 **4** **Listen again and answer the questions.**

1 How long has James lived in New York City? ....
2 What does James say about stores near his apartment? ....
3 What does Anthony think are bad things about New York City? ....
4 What does Julie like doing on the subway train? ....
5 What did Julie find last week? ....

A Song 4 U Waterloo Sunset

41 **5** **Listen and sing.**

river
cross
friends
night
home
busy
at
paradise

Dirty old [1]........................ , must you keep rolling
Flowing into the night?
People so [2]........................ , makes me feel dizzy
Taxi light shines so bright.
But I don't need no [3]........................ .
As long as I gaze on Waterloo sunset
I am in paradise.

Chorus
Every day I look [4]........................ the world from
my window,
But chilly, chilly is the evening time,
Waterloo sunset's fine.

Terry meets Julie, Waterloo station
Every Friday [5]........................ .
But I am so lazy, don't want to wander
I stay at [6]........................ at night.
But I don't feel afraid,
As long as I gaze on Waterloo sunset
I am in paradise.

Chorus

Millions of people swarming like flies round
Waterloo Underground,
But Terry and Julie [7]........................ over the
river
Where they feel safe and sound.
And they don't need no friends,
As long as they gaze on Waterloo sunset,
They are in [8]........................ .
Waterloo sunset's fine.

Writing for your Portfolio

6 Read the letter. Then write a short letter to an English-speaking friend.

THE SHERIDAN HOTEL
1400 88TH AVENUE
QUEENS VILLAGE
NY 16211-1000

4/8/10

Hi Sam,

Here I am in New York City! It's such a fantastic city. We're staying in a nice hotel and the weather's good, too. Yesterday we went to The Empire State Building. The ride to the top was great and the view was really cool!

Today we had lunch at the Hard Rock Café and tomorrow we're going to Central Park. There's a concert there. We have another three days here and I'm going to have a lot more fun! I want to see a show on Broadway!

Do you know what the best thing here is? The food—everything we've eaten has been delicious! I love it here!

See you soon!

Jeanie

7 Work with a partner. Discuss what you like about the place you live.

UNIT 5   51

A history of the U.S. capital

Key words

capital	service	protesters	international
fired	governor	unique	vibrant
Congress	defend	capitol	population

1 **Read the text. Write down three interesting facts about Washington, D.C. Compare them with a partner.**

After more than 200 years as the U.S. capital, Washington, D.C., remains a unique city with more to offer than just government buildings.

The first capital

Philadelphia was the first American capital city. In the nation's early days, Congress met at Independence Hall in Philadelphia. Then, in 1783, a mob of soldiers went to Independence Hall to protest. They wanted to be paid for their service during the American Revolutionary War. Congress asked the governor of Pennsylvania to defend Congress against the protesters. But the governor did not do as Congress asked. And so Congress had to leave Philadelphia. It was at that point that the government decided to create a new capital in a new place. Congress would rule over the new city as well as the nation.

Early Washington, D.C.

George Washington, the first president of the United States, decided to move the nation's capital to Washington, D.C. In 1791, President Washington appointed Pierre Charles L'Enfant to design the new city. L'Enfant, who was born in France, based his design on the city of Paris. But after a year of working on the design, Washington fired L'Enfant. Andrew Ellicott then took over the design of the city. By 1800 the U.S. government moved to its new city.

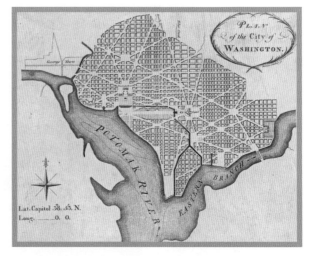

A landmark city

Washington, D.C., lies on the Potomac River between the states of Virginia and Maryland. The "D.C." stands for "District of Columbia." Planners built the city in a square shape. Each side of the square was 10 miles long. The design included the Capitol and the White House, plus Pennsylvania Avenue.

The War of 1812

During the War of 1812, Washington, D.C., was attacked. The War of 1812 was fought between the U.S. and Great Britain. It lasted from 1812 to 1815. The attack on Washington, D.C., became known as the Burning of Washington. The attack destroyed many buildings, including the White House. The United States won the War of 1812, and the White House was rebuilt. By 1817, the U.S. president had moved back in.

Washington, D.C., today

Today Washington, D.C., is an international, vibrant city. It has a population of almost 600,000 people. In addition, about 15 million people visit Washington, D.C., every year, and 1.2 million of them are international visitors.

Many visitors come to see Washington, D.C.'s famous sites. For example, each year 7 million people visit the Smithsonian National Museum of Natural History. Six million people visit the National Air & Space Museum. Three million people visit the National Museum of American History.

Mini-project My capital city

2

Write a report about the history of the capital city of the country where you live. Use the example of Washington, D.C., above as a model. Choose a certain period in your country's history. Write a short text. You could include:

- How many people lived there.
- Who the ruler of the country was.
- Any historic events that took place at the time.
- What life was like for the citizens of the city.
- Pictures to illustrate the text.

You could present the information in the form of a diary. Imagine that you are someone living in the city at the time you have chosen.

1 **Read the text and answer the questions.**

In this unit

You learn
- simple present passive
- *make* and *let*
- words for jobs

and then you can
- talk about ambition
- say where things are done
- say what people let you do

We built this igloo.

They are only around in the summer.

Canada's really beautiful.

Snowmobiling is fun!

Hi! My name's Curtis. I live near Whitehorse, Canada, a town with a population of about 20,000 people. My dad's a Mountie, a police officer with the Royal Canadian Mounted Police, and my mother's a dentist.

In winter it's very cold in Whitehorse, and there's a lot of snow. I love the winter. I have a lot of fun riding on my snowmobile. I've got a really cool one, it's called a Ski-Doo and it's made in Canada. But I am not allowed to drive too far into the woods. My mom thinks I'll get lost out there. Last year Dad helped me and my friend Charlie build an igloo on the frozen Yukon River. The best thing was that our parents let us spend a night in the igloo. We weren't afraid because the grizzly bears aren't around in the winter. That's when they're all hibernating. But I think our parents were worried anyway, because they picked us up very early in the morning.

When it snows a lot, my dad makes me shovel the snow in front of the house and garage. I don't have to do much housework, but my parents make me keep my bedroom clean.

My room's pretty big. I have a computer in it, plus a stereo and a television. My parents let me watch TV until 9:30, when I have to turn it off. There's one other thing they don't let me do—listen to my stereo at full volume when they are home. They say my music gives them a headache!

2 **Answer the questions.**

1 What do Curtis' parents do?
2 Why isn't Curtis allowed to go too far into the woods?
3 Why weren't Curtis and Charlie scared of the grizzly bears?
4 What does Curtis have to do when it snows a lot?
5 What does he have in his bedroom?

Get talking Saying where things are done

42

3 **Listen and match the pictures with the countries.**

1 Switzerland
2 Germany
3 Brazil, Portugal
4 Italy, France
5 United States
6 Indonesia, Africa, India
7 Japan
8 South America
9 China

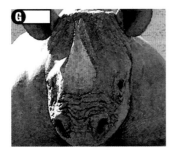

4 **Cover up Exercise 3. Ask and answer questions with a partner.**

Where is	Portuguese German the yen the yuan	spoken? used?
Where are	Porsches Hollywood movies swatches	made?
	truffles rhinos llamas	found?

Language Focus

Vocabulary Jobs

43 **1** **Match the words and the pictures. Listen and check.**

1 writer
2 mechanic
3 nurse
4 salesclerk
5 police officer
6 computer
   programmer
7 waiter
8 electrician
9 doctor
10 dentist

2 **What is important to you in a job? Put these things in order (1 = most important, 10 = least important).**

☐ working outdoors   ☐ being independent   ☐ earning a good salary
☐ being creative   ☐ being with people   ☐ working with children
☐ helping people   ☐ wearing a uniform   ☐ having a lot of responsibility
☐ fixing things

Sounds right /ɪ/ vs. /iː/

44 **3** **Listen and repeat.**

> be   it   eat   is   easy   live   leave   give   teach   in   Portuguese

1 It isn't easy to live here.   4 Give it to him when you leave.
2 Eat it quickly, please.   5 She wants to live in Brazil and teach Portuguese.
3 He is going to live in Italy.

Get talking Talking about ambition

4 **Work with a partner. Discuss what you want to be and why.**

A What do you want to be?

B A teacher.

A Why?

B Because I like working with children and helping others. What about you?

Grammar

Simple present passive

1 **Look at the text on page 54 and complete the examples.**

It's a Ski-Doo and it [1]......... [2].................. in Canada.
I [3]........ [4].................. .... to drive too far into the woods.

2 **Complete the table.**

Affirmative
Portuguese [1].................. **spoken** in Brazil and Portugal.
A lot of watches [2].................. **made** in Switzerland.
Negative
Spanish [3].................. **spoken** in Canada.
These cassette players [4].................. **produced** any more.
Questions and short answers
[5].................. this watch **made** in China? **Yes, it is. / No, it isn't.**
[6].................. those watches **made** in Switzerland? **Yes, they are. / No, they aren't.**

We use the passive when we talk about actions and when it is not clear or important who the action is carried out by. You can add *by* + object to specify who the action is carried out by.

3 **Read the sentences and circle A (Active) or P (Passive) for each one.**

1 Hockey is played in many countries.   A/P
2 This watch is not made any more.   A/P
3 They play hockey in many countries.   A/P
4 They don't make this watch any more.   A/P

4 **Complete the sentences with the simple present passive of the verbs on the right.**

1 Some new songs are only ...*sold*.... on the Internet.
2 Music .... illegally every day from the Internet.
3 In Africa, more than 1,000 languages ....
4 In some countries, insects .... for food.
5 Chocolate .... from cocoa beans.
6 The dollar .... in the U.S.

speak
download
use
~~sell~~
eat
make

5 **Reorder the words to make questions in the simple present passive. Then write short answers.**

1 Portuguese / spoken / in India / is?   **A:** *Is Portuguese spoken in India* ?   **B:** *No, it isn't*
2 olive oil / is / used / in Italy?   **A:** ....?   **B:** ....
3 in Brazil / are / driven / snowmobiles?   **A:** ....?   **B:** ....
4 snow / is / found / in Kenya?   **A:** ....?   **B:** ....

make and *let*

6 **Circle the correct word. Then check against the text on page 54.**

Our parents ¹*made / let* us spend a night in the igloo. My dad ²*makes / lets* me shovel the snow...
My parents ³*make / let* me keep my bedroom clean. My parents ⁴*make / let* me watch TV until 9:30...

Now look at the question and negative form.

Do your parents *make / let* you stay out late? **Yes, they do. / No, they don't.**

7 **Complete the rules with *make* or *let*.**

To say that someone is allowed to do something, use ¹........................ + object + verb.
To say that someone has to do something, use ²........................ + object + verb.

8 **Complete the sentences with *make / makes / made* or *let / lets*.**

1 Yesterday my biology teacher .....*made*..... me stay after class for half an hour.
2 My dad often .... me take out the garbage.
3 When I get good grades, my mom .... me use her computer.
4 I hope Ms. Simmons doesn't .... us study all those words.
5 My friend wouldn't .... me use his MP3 player yesterday.
6 Last week our English teacher .... us watch a great DVD.

Get talking   Saying what people let you do

45 **9** **Listen and match the phrases with the pictures.**

1 talk on my cell phone for hours
2 drink soft drinks
3 dye your hair
4 buy your own clothes

5 have parties at your house
6 watch TV after nine o'clock
7 ride your bike without a helmet
8 go to dance clubs

10 **Work in pairs. Ask and answer questions about John and Angela.**

A Do John's parents let him ride his bike without a helmet?

B Yes, they do. / No, they don't.

Skills

Reading

1 **Read the text below from a teen magazine. Match the interviewer's questions with the girl's answers.**

A Where do you and your friends hang out?
B Can you tell me something about your family?
C Do you live in an apartment or a house?
D What languages do you speak?

TEENS TODAY

Interviewer: [1] ☐

Milase: At home we speak KwaZulu, but at school we speak English most of the time because all subjects are taught in English. When my parents were children, they weren't allowed to speak KwaZulu at school. That was in the days of apartheid.

Interviewer: [2] ☐

Milase: Well, my father's a waiter in a hotel and my mother works in a store.

I have three brothers. They are 6, 8, and 11.

Interviewer: [3] ☐

Milase: We live in a small house. We have a small yard and we've put big rocks around it as a fence.

Interviewer: [4] ☐

Milase: There is not much to do here, but there is a youth club next to the church. That's where I go on Saturdays and Sundays. But my parents don't let me go

out when it's dark outside. They say it's too dangerous.

Interviewer: Thank you for the interview, Milase.

Milase: You're welcome.

Did you know?

Apartheid was a policy in South Africa that treated non-white people unfairly. It went on from 1948 until 1990.

2 **Match the sentence halves.**

1 Milase speaks
2 Milase's mother
3 Milase is not allowed to
4 Milase goes to a youth club
5 It is dangerous

a works in a store.
b on Saturdays and Sundays.
c two languages.
d go out when it's dark.
e in the area where Milase lives.

Listening

46 **3** **Listen to Diego's story and circle T (True), or F (False) for the sentences below.**

1 When Diego was 14, he went to Mexico for the first time. T / F
2 Diego and his dad crossed the border to work on a farm. T / F
3 When he crossed the border, he had to hide under the seat of a car. T / F
4 Diego was not allowed to watch TV on the farm. T / F
5 Diego likes it in the U.S. T / F
6 Now Diego's family lives in the U.S. T / F

Speaking

4 **Work in pairs. Talk about some of the things your parents *make* and *let* you do.**

A My dad makes me do my homework before I watch TV.
B My mom lets me cook.

Writing for your Portfolio

5 **Read Maria's text about her family. Check the four things she writes about.**

There are four of us in our family: my mom, my dad, my brother, and me. My brother is 19. He is an electrician. My father's 42 and he's a police officer, and my mother is 40 and she's a nurse.
We live in a small house with a yard. Our house has three bedrooms, so my brother and I each have our own rooms.
When I go out during the week, I have to be home by nine o'clock. When I go to a party on the weekend, I have to be back by midnight. I also have to keep my room clean.

1 coming home ☐
2 physical descriptions ☐
3 where other people live ☐
4 who is in her family ☐
5 her house ☐
6 ages / jobs of people in her family ☐

6 **Write a short text about your own family. Start by writing a list of things you want to include. Use the ideas from Exercise 5 to help you. Then write your text.**

Check your progress Units 5 and 6

1 **Complete the sentences.**

1 You can see shows at the t _ _ _ _ _ _ .
2 There is an exhibition at the m _ _ _ _ _ .
3 There is a c _ _ _ _ _ _ in the park tonight.
4 There is a game on at the s_ _ _ _ _ _ .
5 We bought some fruit at the
    f_ _ _ _ _ ' _ m _ _ _ _ _ .
6 You can buy everything in a s _ _ _ _ s _ _ _ _ .
7 There are a lot of fish at the a _ _ _ _ _ _ _ .

☐ **7**

2 **Complete the sentences. Use the passive.**

1 Ford cars .... (make) in Detroit.
2 .... baseball .... (play) in the U.S.?
3 Portuguese .... (speak) in Brazil.
4 These cars ....(not/produce) any more.
5 .... CDs .... (sell) on the Internet?

☐ **5**

3 **Complete the dialogues. Use question tags.**

A You're the boy who lives at 3955,
¹ ....?

B Yes, I am. You lived at 3935,
² ....?

A Yes, we moved last year.

B You were at my school, ³ ....?

A Yes, but I go to a different school now.

A This math homework is easy, ⁴ ....?

B No, it's not. You will help me, ⁵ ....?

A He doesn't have a new bike, ⁶ ....?

B Yes, he does. He bought it yesterday.

A They are English, ⁷ ....?

B No, I think they're American. They were
    born in the U.S., ⁸ ....?

☐ **8**

4 **Complete the sentences with a relative pronoun.**

1 That's the car .... he bought.
2 He's the man .... taught us last year.
3 That's the book .... I'm going to buy
    tomorrow.
4 Ford is a company .... makes cars.
5 She's the girl .... won the competition.

☐ **5**

5 **Complete the sentences with the correct job.**

1 He fixes lights. He's an e _ _ _ _ _ _ _ _ _ _ _ .
2 He helps people who are sick. He's a n _ _ _ _ .
3 He fixes people's teeth. He's a d _ _ _ _ _ _ .
4 He works in a garage. He's a m _ _ _ _ _ _ _ .
5 His books are famous. He's a w _ _ _ _ _ .
6 He works in a café. He's a w _ _ _ _ _ .
7 He works with computers.
    He's a c _ _ _ _ _ _ _ p _ _ _ _ _ _ _ _ .
8 She sells things. She's a s _ _ _ _ _ _ _ _ _ .
9 He works in a hospital. He's a d _ _ _ _ _ .
10 She helps people. She's a p _ _ _ _ _ o _ _ _ _ _ _ .

☐ **10**

6 **Write the questions.**

1 ....
    Yes, we have tickets for the 9:00 p.m. show.
2 ....
    The movie is two hours long.
3 ....
    Yes, the supermarket is open on Sundays.
4 ....
    I want to be a teacher.
5 ....
    A student ticket is $3.50.

☐ **10**

7 **Complete the text with the correct form of *make* or *let*.**

Mark's parents ¹ .... him stay up late on
weekends, but during the week they ² ....
him go to bed early. Last week, they ³ ....
him go to bed at 9:00 p.m. every night because
he had exams. On the weekend, his mother
usually ⁴ .... him clean his room, but she
also ⁵ .... him use the car to go and see
friends.

☐ **5**

TOTAL	50

My progress so far is ...

☺ great! ☐   😐 good. ☐   ☹ poor. ☐

English around the world

1 **Read about different forms of English and answer the questions.**

English is spoken as a native language by about 375 million people around the world. Another 750 million people speak it as a foreign language. There are now more non-native speakers of English than there are native speakers. Millions of Chinese children study English, and you can't get into college in China without passing an English exam. The new English speakers are changing the language and new forms of English are developing around the world. For example, the English spoken in the Philippines is "Englog," and "Japlish" is spoken in Japan. "Italglish" is spoken by the Italian immigrant population in the U.S. And there is also Chinglish, Russlish, Spanglish, and Hinglish. For example, *Hungry kya?* meaning *Are you hungry?* appeared on an advertisement for a pizza chain in India. Each nationality adds new words and expressions to the language and pronounces and uses it in their own way. Why do people want to learn English? One reason may be because the world needs a common language for communicating. Today that language is English, but who knows – maybe tomorrow it will be Chinese, Bengali, or Malay.

1 How many people speak English as a foreign language?
2 Who speaks Italglish?
3 What does *Hungry kya?* mean?
4 Which nationalities do you think speak Chinglish, Russlish, Spanglish, and Hinglish?

47 **2** **Look at the sign in English and another language. Which other language do you think it is? Listen and check. Then complete the summary below.**

Canada is a bilingual country. It has two languages, [1]............ and [2]............ .
In Quebec, French is used on [3]............ and in the media. At school, children learn [4]............ and French is the main language for about 80 percent of the population. It is the second most common [5]............ in Canada after English.

3 **Over 2 U!** **Discuss the questions below with a partner.**

When do you use English?
Have you seen any strange signs, advertisements, or menu translations that combine English and another language?

Do you know?

As more Italian immigrants moved to the U.S., an area of New York City became known as "Little Italy." Today, you can find a "Little Italy" in just about every major city in the U.S., as well as other ethnic neighborhoods.

MORE! Now you can watch Episode 3 of *The School Magazine!*

Burundi boy

Children's Express reporter Nestor Sayo left war-torn Burundi in 1995. Now, he says, he's making the most of his new life.

Even though I've spent most of my life in the U.S., I still think a lot about Burundi in Africa, because it's where I was born. A lot of people think that I've forgotten about Burundi because I was only four years old when I left. But I always tell them, there are things I'll always remember.

Burundi was once a peaceful place, but it turned into a battlefield. That is why we left. I was very happy before war broke out between the Tutsi and Hutu people. I was part of a very big family with lots of aunts, uncles, and cousins. But many of them, children and grown-ups, were killed in the fighting.

When my mother and I left Burundi, we traveled on a bus for eight hours to Uganda. It was so tiring and all we had to eat was two slices of bread. We were only in Uganda for a short time before moving on to Kenya, where we stayed for a few months.

One day my mother took me to the airport and told me we were going to catch a plane. I didn't even know which country we'd end up in. We landed and I found out we were in America.

It was December, right in the middle of winter. Coming from Africa, I was freezing. The first few weeks of my new life were spent in a hotel. Then we got sent to a hotel for refugee families. There were a lot of people at the hotel from all over the world—from China, India, Brazil, and Africa.

I couldn't speak English, but it didn't take me long to pick up words such as "Hello." My mom knew only three words: "No English" and "Sorry."

In some ways, I think of the U.S. as being "home" now. I've made many friends here and I'm just as proud of this country as anyone born here.

Sometimes I miss Burundi, but some of my family are still living there. I know I'll go back and visit them. Maybe one day I'll even be able to buy a house there.

For **MORE!** Go to www.cambridge.org/elt/americanmore and take a quiz on this text.

In this unit

You learn
- *used to*
- *so do I / neither do I*
- words for music

and then you can
- talk about what you used to do
- agree and disagree

48

1 Read and listen to the dialogue.

Claire Listen to that! How funny! I can't believe I used to like them.

Karen Who is it? I can't even remember them.

Rick Neither can I, and I had to listen to all of Claire's music when I was younger!

Claire It's *Don't Speak* by No Doubt.

Karen Oh, yes! That's what it is! I remember it now.

Oliver So do I. You used to play this all the time.

Claire Don't remind me! So, what else do we have here?

Oliver Pink, Outkast, I didn't use to like U2, but now I'm a big fan.

In fact, I have a lot of their CDs. So, what are you into right now, Rick?

Rick I like hip-hop, especially classic stuff. I've just borrowed a bunch of my brother's old music. He used to spend his allowance on CDs, so he has a massive collection.

Claire I used to spend all my money on music, but now I've started collecting recorded books. You can get some amazing books!

Karen That's a great idea. Do you have *Lord of the Rings*?

Claire Yes, I have it on my MP3 player!

Answer the questions.

1 Who used to like No Doubt?
2 Who is a U2 fan?
3 What kind of music does Rick like at the moment?
4 What did Rick's brother use to do with his allowance?
5 What kind of collection does Claire have?
6 Has she always collected these things?

Get talking Talking about what you used to do

 Listen and repeat.

Interviewer Which TV show did you use to watch when you were 10?
Girl I used to watch *Charmed*!

Interviewer What did you use to like when you were younger?
Boy I used to like roller skating.

 Match the questions and answers. Then listen and check.

 Questions

1 Dad, what music did you listen to when you were young?
2 Grandma, did you watch a lot of TV when you were a girl?
3 How did you use to spend your Saturdays, Mom?
4 Did you use to read a lot, John?
5 What was your favorite TV show back then, Natasha?

Answers

a Not really. I didn't like TV. I used to read.
b When I was younger, I used to watch *Buffy*!
c I used to like a band called Talking Heads.
d No, I used to go to the movies a lot.
e I used to go dancing on Saturdays!

5 **Work in pairs. Ask each other questions about what you used to do when you were younger.**

A What shows did you use to watch when you were younger?

B I used to watch cartoons all the time!

Language Focus

Vocabulary Music

1 Number the musical styles (1 = your favorite, 13 = your least favorite).

☐ Dance ☐ R&B ☐ Folk ☐ Indie

☐ Hip-hop ☐ Opera ☐ Pop ☐ Jazz ☐ Country

☐ Blues ☐ Rock ☐ Heavy metal ☐ Classical

Get talking Agreeing and disagreeing

51

2 Complete the dialogue with the phrases on the left. Listen and check.

Oh, I do
Neither do I
So do I

Richard Do you like dance music?

Susan No, I don't.

Richard ¹..................................... , but my sister does. She's got hundreds of dance CDs.

Susan So what do you like?

Richard Well, post-punk bands like The Killers.

Susan ²..................................... . Have you got any Green Day CDs too?

Richard Yes, but I don't like them that much.

Susan ³.................... . I really do.

3 Work with a partner. Talk about the music you like or dislike.

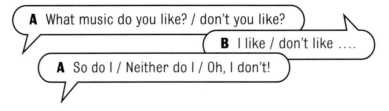

A What music do you like? / don't you like?

B I like / don't like ....

A So do I / Neither do I / Oh, I don't!

Grammar

used to

1 **Complete the sentences. Then check against the dialogue on page 64.**

You ¹ .... this all the time.
He ² .... his allowance on CDs, so he has a massive collection.
I ³ .... U2, but now I'm a big fan.

We use *used to / didn't use to* (+ verb) to talk about past habits.
The question (*Did you use to ...?*) is almost never used.

2 **Put the words in the correct order.**

1 live / there / I / to / used ....*I used to live there.*..........................
2 to my school / used / go / She / to ....
3 the U.S. / to / We / live / used / in ....
4 to / vegetables / didn't / eat / I / use ....
5 have / didn't / to / I / use / my own bedroom ....
6 rock / didn't / like / My father / to / use / music ....

3 **Complete with one of the phrases on the right.**

1 I ....*didn't use to speak*....... English, but now I can say some things.
2 Steve .... the guitar at all, but now he plays very well.
3 My brother hates pizza, but when he was younger he .... it every day.
4 My mother .... Spanish, but now she's forgotten it.
5 We never go to the movies these days, but we .... every weekend.
6 My parents .... on vacation, but now they take a trip every year.
7 My favorite player is Alex Rodriguez. He .... for the Texas Rangers.
8 I .... spinach, but now I really love it!

used to eat
didn't use to eat
used to play
didn't use to play
used to go
didn't use to go
used to speak
~~didn't use to speak~~

4 **Complete with *used to* or *didn't use to* and a verb from the box.**

~~speak~~	eat	wear	live	be	do

1 My father ....*used to speak*.. some Japanese, but now he's forgotten it all.
2 My sister .... only white clothes, but now she likes to wear a lot of colors.
3 My brother .... a nervous person, but he isn't any more.
4 I .... any exercise, but now I run four times a week.
5 I .... vegetables, but now I eat them all the time.
6 We .... in a really small apartment, but now we live in a big house.

so do I / neither do I

⑤ Complete the examples. Then check against the dialogue on page 64.

Karen I remember it now.
Oliver ¹ .... You used to play this all the time.
Karen I can't even remember them.
Rick ² ...., and I had to listen to them when I was younger.

We use these phrases to <u>agree</u> with what another person says.
Simple present
If the other person says something affirmative, use: *So do I.*
If the other person says something negative, use: *Neither do I.*
Other verbs
"I**'m** tired." "**So am I.**"   "I **can't** sing." "**Neither can I.**"   "I arrived late." "**So did I.**"

⑥ Complete the dialogues with these phrases.

So do I.	So did I.	~~So can I.~~	So have I.
Neither do I.	Neither did I.	Neither can I.	Neither have I.

1 **A** Look! I can walk on my hands!
  B .... *So can I!* ....
2 **A** This homework's hard. I can't do it.
  B ....
3 **A** I have a new bike.
  B ....
4 **A** I always go to the movies on Fridays.
  B ....

5 **A** We enjoyed ourselves at the party.
  B ....
6 **A** I've never been to Europe.
  B ....
7 **A** I didn't go out last night.
  B ....
8 **A** My sister doesn't like rap.
  B ....

> I can walk on my hands!

> So can I!

⑦ Complete the replies.

1 I love spaghetti!   ...*So do I.*...
2 My brother has an MP3 player.   ....
3 I went to Florida last year.   ....
4 I don't know the answer.   ....

5 I'm sorry, I can't go out tonight. ....
6 She didn't pass the test.   ....
7 Mary can sing opera.   ....

⑧ Find sentences you agree with. Write *So ... I* or *Neither ... I*. Compare your answers with a partner's answers.

1 I'm 16.   ....
2 I'm not interested in sports.   ....
3 I love football.   ....
4 I watched TV last night.   ....
5 I read magazines a lot.   ....
6 I can't speak Spanish.   ....

7 I didn't enjoy myself last night. ....
8 I can walk on my hands.   ....
9 I think hip-hop is great.   ....
10 I was in school yesterday.   ....
11 I wasn't home on Sunday.   ....
12 I haven't been to Canada.   ....

Reading

1 Read and listen. Match the photos to the paragraphs.

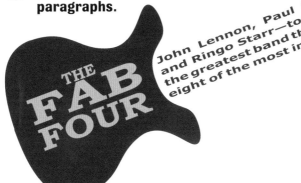

John Lennon, Paul McCartney, George Harrison, and Ringo Starr—together they were The Beatles, the greatest band the world has ever seen. Here are eight of the most important events in their history.

Lennon and McCartney meet

On July 6, 1957, fifteen-year-old Paul McCartney first met John Lennon in Liverpool. John Lennon was on stage with his band The Quarry Men. Later in the evening, Paul played piano with the band. They thought he was so good that they asked him to join them.

The Beatles go to Germany ¹☐

In August 1960, The Beatles went to Germany, where they played at Hamburg's Star Club until December 1. The band was made up of John Lennon (rhythm guitar/vocals), Paul McCartney (rhythm/vocals), George Harrison (lead guitar/vocals), and two other musicians on the bass and the drums.

The early hits ²☐

In summer 1962, a new drummer, Ringo Starr, joined John, Paul, and George. On October 11, 1962, the Beatles made their first appearance in the U.K. charts with "Love Me Do." In early 1963, their second single "Please Please Me" became their first number 1. The Beatles quickly followed this with another number 1 single, "From Me to You," and a number 1 album, also named *Please Please Me.*

The Beatles "invade" the U.S. ³☐

On February 7, 1964, 10,000 fans were at New York's Kennedy Airport to see Pan-Am flight PA101 land. On board were Paul, John, George, and Ringo. Four days later, The Beatles played their first American concert in Washington, D.C., to 8,600 screaming fans. More than 70 million Americans watched their performance on TV. On April 4, 1964, the top five singles in the United States were "Can't Buy Me Love," "Twist and Shout," "She Loves You," "I Want to Hold your Hand," and "Please Please Me"—all of them were Beatles songs!

Sergeant Pepper's Lonely Hearts Club Band

On June 1, 1967, The Beatles released their eighth album, *Sergeant Pepper's Lonely Hearts Club Band.* Many people think this is the greatest of all their records. The album had the famous songs "She's Leaving Home," "When I'm Sixty-Four" and "Lucy in the Sky with Diamonds." It was also famous for its cover, which showed pictures of many of the band's idols.

The last show

On January 30, 1969, The Beatles played their last concert. It was a show on the roof of their record company in London. A large group of fans watched from the street below, but there were complaints about the noise from neighbors so the police arrived and stopped the show after only 42 minutes. Just over a year later, the band broke up.

The death of John Lennon ⁴☐

On December 8, 1980, when John Lennon was outside his home in New York City with his wife, Yoko Ono, a crazed fan called Mark Chapman shot him. John's death was a great shock all over the world. Now people knew that The Beatles would never play together again.

The release of *One* ⁵☐

In November 2000, a compilation of The Beatles' number 1 hits called *One* went straight to the top of the album charts. It was the fastest selling CD of the year and sold 320,000 copies in the first week. It also reached number 1 in many other countries around the world, including Germany, France, Spain, and Canada. It showed that The Beatles were still one of the biggest and most popular bands in the world.

2 **Write the questions for these answers.**

1 In Liverpool in 1957. _When and where did Paul first meet John?_

2 In August 1960. ....

3 "Please Please Me." ....

4 10,000. ....

5 In the summer of 1962. ....

6 On the roof of their record company. ....

Listening

 3 **Paul Sacks and Sally Green are critics on the hit TV talent show *Superstar*. Listen and write the name of the person these sentences refer to (Jasmine or Dave).**

1 Your voice needs a little more training. ....

2 You're not going to be our next superstar. ....

3 You look fantastic. ....

4 You gave it a try and that's what's important. ....

5 We certainly want to talk to you again. ....

6 You were out of tune. ....

Speaking

2

4 Work in pairs. Listen to these three performers and say what you think.

 Steve   Tina   Jeff

… looks fantastic / doesn't look like a pop star.
…'s got a beautiful / terrible voice / needs (doesn't need) training.
… is an excellent singer / was out of tune / has(n't) got what it takes.
… could be the next pop star / is never going to make it as a pop star / is(n't) on the way up.

Writing for your Portfolio

5 Read the text and put the headings in the correct places.

Career
Full name
Why I like her music
Born

My favorite singer

1 .... : Beyoncé Giselle Knowles

2 .... : Houston, Texas, in 1981

3 .... : Beyoncé rose to fame as a member of the band Destiny's Child. Their records sold millions of copies. In 2003 Beyoncé released her first solo album, *Dangerously in Love*. In 2006 she starred in the movies *The Pink Panther* and *Dreamgirls*.

4 .... : I love Beyoncé's music because she has an excellent voice and she is a great performer. My favorite Beyoncé songs are "Beautiful Liar" and "Irreplaceable."

6 Now write a short summary about a pop star / band that you like.

Musical instruments

Key words

bamboo	folk music	metallic	an opening
binding	pear-shaped body	stringed	

1 Look at the pictures of the four musical instruments.

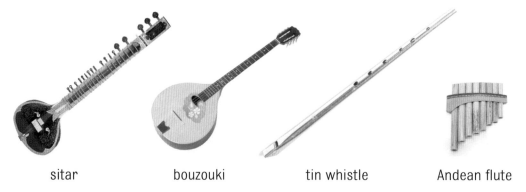

sitar   bouzouki   tin whistle   Andean flute

2 Listen. Guess which instrument you hear. Write the numbers next to the names of the instruments.

sitar ....   bouzouki ....   tin whistle ....   Andean flute ....

3 Write the names of the instruments from above into the text.

The [1].. comes from Ecuador and is made of bamboo. It has 7 notes and is very easy to play. It often has a decorative binding.

The [2].. is important in modern Greek music as well as in other Balkan folk music. It is a stringed instrument with a pear-shaped body and a very long neck. The instrument has a sharp metallic sound.

The [3].. is a simple wind instrument with six holes. It can be made out of different kinds of metal. It is popular in traditional Irish music. Many children in Ireland play it because it doesn't cost much to buy and is easy to learn.

The [4].. is probably the best-known South Asian instrument in the West. It is an Indian classical stringed instrument. It became popular in the West when The Beatles used it in their songs. It is difficult to play.

4 Folk music across the continents: The extracts you are going to hear are from Australia, Asia, North America, South America, and Europe. Try to guess where they are from.

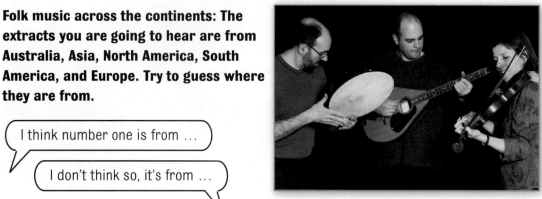

> I think number one is from ...

> I don't think so, it's from ...

5 Look at the orchestra. Label the different sections.

a) woodwind   b) brass   c) percussion   d) string

¹ The .... section.

² The .... section.

³ The .... section.

⁴ The .... section.

6 Listen to the three following pieces of classical music. Which instruments can you hear?

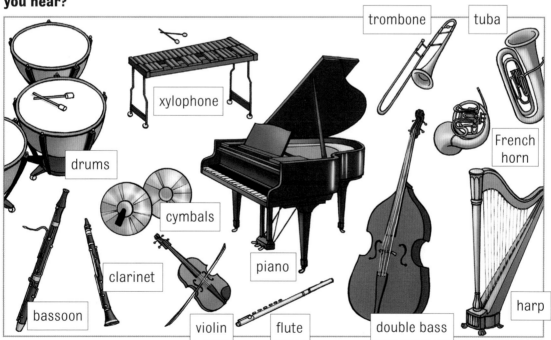

trombone

tuba

xylophone

drums

French horn

cymbals

piano

clarinet

violin   flute

double bass

harp

bassoon

Mini-project Instruments from around the world

7 Find out about two unusual instruments from your country.
Write a short text about each one. Include a picture.

8 Natural disasters

1 **Read the text. Write the words in italics under the correct picture.**

http://www.historynews.net

Great disasters of the modern world

1

3

2

4

1 At 7:58 local time on December 26, 2004, a huge undersea earthquake took place in the Indian Ocean near the western coast of the Indonesian island of Sumatra. *The earthquake created tsunamis* that quickly traveled toward the coasts of several different countries, including Indonesia and Thailand to the east, Bangladesh to the north, and India, Sri Lanka, and the African countries of Kenya and Somalia to the west. Warnings were sent, but they arrived too late. Many of the coasts of these countries were hit by huge waves up to 15 meters high. Buildings and even *complete villages were destroyed.* Almost 300,000 people were killed.

2 On Tuesday, January 12, 2010, the people of Haiti experienced a devastating earthquake. Its epicenter was about 25 kilometers west of Port-au-Prince, the capital of Haiti. *Many important historical buildings were damaged or destroyed.* Dozens of strong aftershocks occurred in the days and weeks following the earthquake. More than 150,000 people lost their lives in the quake, which affected more than 3 million people. *Many countries sent aid to help the quake's survivors.*

In this unit

You learn
- *too / not ... enough*
- past passive
- words for catastrophes

and then you can
- express sympathy
- explain things in simpler words
- talk about when people were born

2 **Circle T (True) or F (False) for the sentences below.**

1 The Indian Ocean disaster took place in November 2004. T / F
2 Countries on four continents were affected by the Indian Ocean tsunami. T / F
3 Almost 300,000 people were killed. T / F
4 No one helped Haiti after the earthquake. T / F
5 More than three million people were affected by the earthquake in Haiti. T / F

Get talking Expressing sympathy

6 **3** **Listen to the conversation. Complete it using the expressions on the right.**

A ¹ ....
A ² ....
A ³ ....
A ⁴ ....

B Not very well.
B It's about our dog.
B It died yesterday.

How are you, Sandra?

What about it?

Oh, I'm so sorry to hear that.

What's the matter?

4 **Choose situations. Act out dialogues like the one above.**

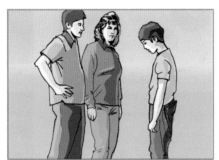

next weekend / I'm not allowed to come to your birthday party

tonight / I can't come to the movie

sister / was taken to the hospital yesterday

best friend / had a bike accident last week

new MP3 player / I broke it this morning

science test / I got a bad grade

Language Focus

Vocabulary Catastrophes

7 **1** **Match the words with their definitions. Then listen and check.**

1 ☐ a lot of water covering a place that is usually dry.
2 ☐ a long time without rain.
3 ☐ a mass of mud and earth sliding down a mountain.
4 ☐ a mountain with a large hole in the top through which lava comes out.
5 ☐ a violent wind, especially found in the western Atlantic Ocean.
6 ☐ an extremely large wave that often happens after an earthquake.
7 ☐ when masses of ice and snow fall quickly down the side of a mountain.
8 ☐ when the earth shakes so strongly that sometimes houses are destroyed.
9 ☐ when a forest starts to burn.

a an earthquake

b an avalanche

c a volcano

d a flood

e a drought

f a tsunami

g a forest fire

h a mudslide

i a hurricane

Get talking Explaining things in simpler words

2 **Cover up Exercise 1. In pairs, ask and answer questions.**

A What's an "earthquake?"

B It's when the earth shakes so strongly that sometimes houses are destroyed.

B What's a "volcano?"

A A volcano? That's a mountain with hot lava inside. The lava comes out through a hole in the top.

Grammar

too / not ... enough

| Warnings were sent but they | arrived **too** late. |
| | did**n't** arrive soon **enough**. |

1 **Complete the sentences with the adjectives on the right.**

good
strong
~~tall~~
tired
late

1 He's not .....*tall*..... enough to get the apple from the tree.
2 We're too .... to see the movie. It started 15 minutes ago.
3 I'm not .... enough to be on the school football team.
4 She's too .... to do her homework now. She should go to bed.
5 You're not .... enough to lift this.

Past passive

2 **Complete the examples with words from the box. Then check against the text on page 74.**

were destroyed   were damaged   were hit
were sent   were killed

Many important historical buildings [1] .... or destroyed.
Warnings [2] ....
Many of the coasts of these countries [3] .... by huge waves.
Complete villages [4] ....
Almost 300,000 people [5] ....

3 **Decide if the sentences are passive or active.**

1 The hurricane destroyed thousands of homes. *active*
2 Breakfast is served until 10:00 a.m.
3 He was paid a lot of money for the photo.
4 We're not very happy with our room.
5 The teacher was 10 minutes late for class.
6 Children under 13 are not allowed in.

4 **Write sentences with the past passive. Use the words below and *by*.**

1 The email / write / Susan   *The email was written by Susan.* ....
2 The cupcakes / make / Fred   ....
3 The race / win / an Ethiopian   ....
4 The children / rescue / the police ....
5 My website / design / my sister   ....
6 The pictures / paint / a famous artist ....

Sounds right /r/

8 **5** **Listen and repeat. Pay attention to the /r/ sound.**

water   earthquake   destroyed
were   erupted

9 **6** **Listen and repeat the sentences.**

What's the matter?
The volcano erupted.
The buildings were destroyed.

Get talking Talking about when people were born

7 **Write the number of the correct word in the pictures.**

1 telephone   3 car   5 nuclear reactor   7 dynamite   9 dishwasher
2 lightbulb   4 jeans   6 windshield wipers   8 signal flare

8 **Write the names of the inventors under the pictures. Then discuss your answers with a partner.**

A

B

C

D

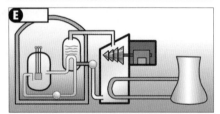

E

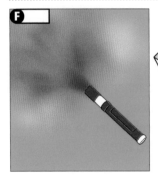

F

G

H

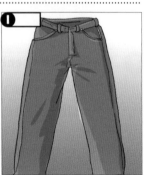

I

Mary Anderson *(born 1866 in Alabama, U.S.)*
Gottlieb Daimler *(born 1834 in Stuttgart, Germany)*
Josephine Cochrane *(born 1839 in Illinois, U.S.)*
Thomas Alva Edison *(born 1847 in Ohio, U.S.)*
Alfred Nobel *(born 1833 in Stockholm, Sweden)*
Levi Strauss *(born 1847 in Bavaria, Germany)*
Enrico Fermi *(born 1901 in Rome, Italy)*

Alexander Graham Bell *(born 1847 in Edinburgh, Scotland)*
Martha Coston *(born 1826 in Baltimore, U.S.)*

A I think the car was invented by Levi Strauss.

B I don't think so. I think it was invented by Gottlieb Daimler. / I think so, too.

Skills

Reading

1 **Read the story.**

CASTAWAY!

1 Chuck's plane was flying over the open ocean when a storm started. The plane ran into trouble when the storm got stronger. ☐

2 Eventually the plane crashed, but Chuck survived and he started swimming. ☐

3 On the island, Chuck learned how to open coconuts to get the milk and which berries were good to eat. ☐

4 After two or three weeks, he opened some of the packages that had washed ashore from the plane's wreckage. ☐

5 ☐ He amused himself by drawing a face on the ball with some of the blood. He gave the ball a name, too.

I know – I'll call you 'Wilson'.

6 ☐ Wilson became Chuck's best friend. When Chuck escaped from the island on a raft six months later, he took Wilson with him.

7 After three days at sea, Wilson fell off the raft, but Chuck couldn't get him back. ☐

8 The following day, several months after the plane crash, a miracle happened. ☐

2 **Write the letters of the extra sentences from the story in the boxes above.**

A He also learned how to catch and cook fish.

B Chuck was rescued and taken back to the United States.

C After swimming for a long time, he reached a desert island.

D The pilot couldn't control the plane.

E Chuck gave up hope and just lay on the raft.

F He was surprised to find a ball in one of them.

G There was no one else to talk to, so Chuck talked to Wilson.

H While he was playing with the ball, Chuck fell down and cut his arm.

Listening

 3 **Listen and find out how Sally and Tom James survived an earthquake. Complete the sentences.**

1 Sally was getting breakfast ready when ....
2 She looked out of the window and saw ....
3 Just before the big quake happened, she ....
4 She shouted and some men came. They ....
5 Tom was on his way ....
6 He stopped his car and ....
7 He ran as fast as he could until he ....
8 When he got back to his car, ...

Speaking

4 **Imagine you are going to spend a year alone on a desert island. You are allowed to take a CD, a book, a DVD, and one other thing with you. Work in pairs. Choose your items and interview each other.**

A What DVD are you going to take?

B I'm going to take *Titanic* because ...

Writing for your Portfolio

5 **Read Paul's story about a forest fire near his home. Then complete it with these words.**

| then | ago | first | When | after | later |

Two years ¹......, there was a bad forest fire near my town. At ²......, it wasn't a problem, but ³...... two days, the firefighters said people had to leave their houses. So we put some clothes into suitcases, and ⁴...... we got in the car and drove to my grandparents' house. Three days ⁵......, the fire stopped, and we drove back to our house. ⁶...... we got there, we saw that the house was OK. We were happy to be back home again!

6 **Write a story about someone who survived an earthquake. Use these verbs and the time words from Exercise 5.**

| to escape | to rescue | to crush | to shake | to collapse | a tremor | safe |

Check your progress Units 7 and 8

1 Complete the words for kinds of music.

1 o _ _ _ _   5 h _ _ _ _ m _ _ _ _
2 f _ _ _   6 d _ _ _ _
3 c _ _ _ _ _ _   7 b _ _ _ _
4 i _ _ _ _   **7**

2 Read the descriptions and complete the words.

1 When there is no rain for a long time.
  a d _ _ _ _ _ _
2 When the earth shakes.
  an e _ _ _ _ _ _ _ _ _
3 When there is too much water.
  a f _ _ _ _
4 Snow and ice that fall down a mountain.
  an a _ _ _ _ _ _ _ _
5 A violent wind.
  a h _ _ _ _ _ _ _ _
6 A mountain with lava inside.
  a v _ _ _ _ _ _   **6**

3 Complete the dialogue with the correct form of *used to*.

A Which school did you ¹....................... go to?
B I ²....................... go to Mansfield School.
A I didn't ³....................... like school, but this year I'm enjoying it.
B That's good. I hope I enjoy this school, too!   **3**

4 Rewrite the sentences using the simple past passive.

1 The hurricane destroyed the forest.
....
2 Van Gogh painted that picture.
....
3 Mark wrote these emails.
....
4 Sarah won the money.
....
5 A carpenter built these houses.
....   **10**

5 Complete the sentences with *too* or *not ... enough*.

1 He is not .... (good) to play for the basketball team.
2 We are .... (late) to see the movie. It started 10 minutes ago.

3 They were not .... (strong) to lift the boxes.
4 I was .... (tired) to stay up late.   **4**

6 Write the questions.

1 .... ?
He was born in 1972.
2 .... ?
Yes, I like jazz.
3 .... ?
I'm sad about my dog.
4 .... ?
It's when the earth shakes.
5 ....?
I'm going to take a good book on vacation.   **10**

7 Complete the dialogues with the correct phrase.

Yes, I do.	So do I.	Do you want
What about	I like	Neither do I.

A Do you like U2?
B ¹...
A That's good. ²...
B ³................................... Green Day?
A I don't like them.
B ⁴...
A ⁵................................... rock music these days. In fact, I'm going to a concert tomorrow.
  ⁶................................... to come?   **6**

What's the matter?	How are you
Not great	I'm so sorry to hear that.

A ⁷..............................., Sue?
B ⁸...
A ⁹...
B It's my grandmother. She's not very well.
A ¹⁰...................................   **4**

   TOTAL   **50**

My progress so far is ...

☺   😐   ☹

great. ☐   good. ☐   poor. ☐

Manga!

1 **Discuss the questions below. Then read the text and answer the questions.**

Do you read manga comics?
Do you watch manga cartoons?
Who is your favorite manga character?

Did you know?

The word *manga* means "comic" in Japanese. Manga is written for both adults and children. The Japanese manga industry is HUGE. It is much bigger than the comic industry in the United States. Yearly sales of manga books and magazines in Japan total about $57 million.

So how did manga start? Cartoon drawing began in Japan almost 800 years ago. Artists drew manga on temple walls. These pictures were very similar to modern manga. In 1702, Shumboko Ono, a famous artist, made a book of these pictures and added captions. Manga artists started to use stories as well as illustrations.

These early comic books were called *Tobae*. They were the main form of literature in Japanese society. In 1947, Tezuka Osamu, a young medical student, created *New Treasure Island*. It was a great success. He became the father of "modern" manga. His most popular work is *Mighty Atom*. He also created *Astro Boy* and *Kimba the White Lion*.

Today in Japan, manga can be found on every street corner. Manga magazines contain at least 200–400 pages of manga in each issue. Hundreds of manga artists work individually or in small groups. Popular manga characters become TV cartoons or animated movies that are watched all over the world.

1 Is manga an old or new art?
2 What is *Tobae*?
3 Who became the father of modern manga?
4 How long are most manga magazines?

11 **2** **Listen and circle the correct word to complete the sentences below.**

1 *Naruto* comes from *a book / a magazine*.
2 *Naruto* takes place in a make-believe world with *five / six* countries.
3 Each country has a hidden *village / city* where Ninja live.
4 The name *Ninja* was the name of *teachers / spies* in the Samurai age.
5 Uzumaki Naruto is a *good / bad* student.
6 He has got an *eight-tailed / nine-tailed* fox inside his body.
7 He has *no / great* strength in times of danger.
8 Naruto's peers *don't possess / all possess* their own special powers.

3  **Work in pairs and design a new manga character. Write an adventure for him or her, then present it to the class.**

MORE! Now you can watch Episode 4 of *The School Magazine!*

HOW TO SURVIVE
Earthquakes

Do you ever get tired of all that advice you get in teen magazines? You know, stuff like how to survive at school, how to survive your parents, how to survive exams—things like that.

Well, I live in San Francisco and here we have something a bit more dangerous than parents and exams. They're called earthquakes and here's my survival guide.

HOW TO SURVIVE
Earthquakes.

Stay calm. If you are inside, first of all get down on the floor and find some cover to protect you from falling objects, such as a heavy table or desk. Stay away from windows and objects that could fall on you. If you are outside, move quickly away from buildings, streetlights, and trees. Try and find an open area.

If you are in a public building, do not rush to the door. That's what everyone else will do. Never use an elevator during an earthquake. After the quake has finished, watch out for aftershocks. These are follow-up quakes. They are usually smaller than the first one but they can still cause damage. They can cause things to fall down.

When you leave your house, make sure you are wearing shoes. There will be a lot of broken glass on the ground, for sure.

So how big was that quake?

The strength of each earthquake is measured on the Richter scale. It goes from 0 to 8.9. Here's a guide to what happens at different levels of the scale.

7.3–8.9
Total destruction;
roads break up and rocks fall.
The ground opens up.

6.2–7.3
People are starting to panic.
Buildings start to fall down.
Water is pushed out of rivers.

4.8–6.2
Now you are finding it difficult
to stand up or walk.
Windows break and tiles
fall off roofs.

4.3–4.8
If you were sleeping, you're
not any more.
Dishes, doors, and trees
shake and rock.

0–4.3
Lying on your bed upstairs,
you are noticing the room is
shaking a bit.
Lights start to swing inside.

For **MORE!** Go to www.cambridge.org/elt/americanmore and take a quiz on this text.

UNIT (9) If I had the money ...

1 Read and listen to the dialogue.

Oliver I really need to buy a new laptop, but don't have enough money.

Claire Why do you need a new laptop?

Oliver Well, if I had a built-in DVD player, I could watch my DVDs anytime, anywhere.

Karen If I were you, I'd use it to do more studying.

Oliver Oh, come on! No one has said anything about my grades. If anyone had, I would have started working harder.

Rick What about Mr. Sweeney?

Oliver What does he know? Everyone knows his classes are hard. I'd work harder if his classes were more interesting. Anyway, if I had this laptop here, I could study anywhere. Look, it's even got wireless LAN.

Karen If you need more money, why don't you get a job?

Oliver Doing what?

Karen Well, if you did a paper route, you'd earn some money.

Rick Hey, I have an idea. There's always someone who needs help with a computer. Why don't you make some money that way?

Oliver Good idea, Rick! Would you like another orange juice?

2 **Match the sentence halves.**

1 Oliver really wants a new laptop
2 He wants to watch DVDs and
3 Karen says he should
4 Oliver thinks he's working
5 If some classes weren't so boring,
6 Rick suggests he helps people
7 Oliver thinks this is

a do more studying.
b by fixing their computers.
c he would work harder.
d but he doesn't have enough money.
e a good idea.
f do a paper route.
g hard enough.

Get talking Giving advice

13

3 **Listen and repeat.**

Girl 1 I need to get more exercise.
Boy 1 If I were you, I'd go running every morning.
Girl 1 Hmm. But I hate running!

Boy 2 I need some extra money.
Girl 2 If I were you, I'd get a job at the mall.
Boy 2 I can't, I'm too young.

4 **Match the expressions and the pictures.**

1 mow the lawn
2 take a dog for a walk
3 wash cars
4 fix computers
5 do a paper route
6 babysit

5 **Work in pairs. Make dialogues like those in Exercise 3.**

A I need …   **B** If I were you, I'd …

Language Focus

Vocabulary Computer words

14 **1** **Write the correct number of the words in the pictures. Listen and check.**

1 CD-ROM	3 mouse	5 laptop	7 modem	9 printer
2 flat screen	4 keyboard	6 DVD	8 flash drive	10 speakers

A
B
C DVD
D
E
F
G
H
I
J

Get talking Talking about people

2 **Work with a partner. Student A says one of the prompts, Student B finishes it. Then switch roles.**

1 I know someone who ....
2 At our school, everyone ....
3 In our class, there isn't anyone who ....
4 In our country, no one ....
5 I don't know anyone who ....
6 At our school, no one is allowed to ....
7 In our class, there is someone who ....
8 In Australia, everyone ....

Grammar

Second conditional

1 Put the verbs into the correct places. Then check against the dialogue on page 84.

were	could watch	had	'd earn	'd work	did

1 I .... harder if his classes .... more interesting.
2 If you .... a paper route, you .... some money.
3 If I .... a built-in DVD player, I .... my DVDs anytime, anywhere.

The second conditional is used to talk about situations that are unreal.
Real: I don't have a notebook. I can't work anywhere.
Unreal: **If** I **had** a notebook, I **could** work anywhere.

Form: **If** clause   **Main clause**
             If + simple past   subject + would/wouldn't or could/couldn't + base form of the verb.

2 Circle the correct word.

1 If I *have / had* more money, I'd buy it for you.
2 If you *go / went* to New York City, you'd learn a lot of English.
3 If it was my birthday today, *I'd get / I got* a lot of presents.
4 I would help you if I *didn't / wouldn't* have homework to do.
5 If he *would have / had* a girlfriend, he'd be very happy.
6 If there was a test tomorrow, I *wouldn't / didn't* pass it.

3 Write the verbs in the correct form.

1 I'd tell you the answer if I ....*knew*.... it myself! (know)
2 If I knew her phone number, I .... her. (call)
3 If today .... Sunday, I'd still be in bed! (be)
4 If you were my friend, you .... me. (help)
5 You'd have more money if you .... a job. (get)

Get talking Talking about what you would do

4 Work in pairs. Look at the prompts. Ask and answer.

A What would you do if you lost your key?

B I'd go to my friend's house. What would you do if ...?

lost your key   were principal of your school   saw your teacher at the school dance
were angry with a friend   saw a famous person   felt sick

If I were you Giving advice

5 **Put the words in the correct order. Then check against the dialogue on page 84.**

If / you / I / I'd / to do more studying / were / use it

This is a special use of the second conditional: we use the phrase **If I were you** to introduce advice for another person.
A I've got toothache.   **B If I were you,** I'd go see a dentist.

6 **Match the sentences.**

1 My tooth hurts.	a If I were you, I'd go for a run.
2 My grades are really bad.	b If I were you, I'd take it to the vet.
3 I need some exercise.	c If I were you, I'd call the repair shop.
4 I'm really tired.	d If I were you, I'd go to the dentist.
5 My dog's sick.	e If I were you, I'd study harder.
6 The television doesn't work.	f If I were you, I'd go to bed early.

Indefinite pronouns *everyone, someone, no one, anyone*

7 **Complete the sentences. Then check against the dialogue on page 84.**

[1] .... has said anything about my grades.
[2] .... knows his classes are hard.
There's always [3] .... who needs help with a computer.
If [4] .... had, I would have started working harder.

- Note that we can also say *everybody / somebody / nobody / anybody*.
- *no one / nobody* is only used with affirmative verb forms.
- *anyone / anybody* can be used with affirmative or negative verb forms:
  Anyone can do this.   *I don't know anybody here.*

8 **Complete the sentences with the correct indefinite pronoun.**

1 We don't need a specialist for this job. ...Anyone.... can do it!
2 When I got to Mike's house, ... was there, so I went home again.
3 I can't do this. I want .... to help me.
4 Everybody is invited. .... can come!
5 I don't know .... who likes her.
6 It was a great party. Mike was there, Jenny was there—....................... was there!

Get talking Asking about how long

> I were you   Everyone in my class

9 **Complete the dialogue with the phrases above. Then listen and check.**

Craig I haven't finished my project yet.
Sonia Really? [1]....................... has already finished.
Craig What can I do? If I had another two days, I'd do a great project.

Sonia If [2]......................., I'd research an idea on the Internet.
Craig Thanks. I'll do that.

Skills

Reading

1 **Read the dilemmas and match them to the pictures.**

Dilemma 1
Imagine your older brother asked you to give him an alibi for last night. He asked you to tell your parents he was with you. What would you do?

Dilemma 2
Imagine someone broke the classroom window when your teacher wasn't there. When she returns, she asks you who it was. What would you do?

Dilemma 3
Imagine you were walking down the street and you found a wallet on the ground. What would you do?

Listening

2 **Listen to Carla and Derek talking about the dilemmas in Exercise 1. Circle T (True) or F (False).**

1 Carla has two brothers. T / F
2 Carla would always give an alibi. T / F
3 Derek has a good relationship with his brother. T / F
4 Carla would definitely tell the teacher. T / F
5 Derek wouldn't tell the teacher anything. T / F
6 Derek thinks it would be unfair if the teacher asked him. T / F
7 Carla would keep the wallet. T / F

Reading and speaking

3 Do the questionnaire. Put a check next to your answers. Then discuss them.

1 Imagine you were at a party. You took a picture off the wall to look at it. You dropped it and it broke. No one saw you do it. What would you do?
- [ ] I'd offer to fix it.
- [ ] I'd put it back on the wall and hope no one would notice.
- [ ] I'd leave it on the floor and go back to the party.

2 Imagine a friend of yours had some new glasses and you thought they looked ridiculous. If your friend asked you for your opinion, what would you do?
- [ ] I would say I liked my friend's old glasses better.
- [ ] I would say they looked ridiculous.
- [ ] I would say they looked good.

3 Imagine you played on the school football team and the team was in the championship. On the day of the game, you woke up and your leg was hurting. What would you do?
- [ ] I'd want to play, so I wouldn't say anything.
- [ ] I'd talk to the coach and ask for advice.
- [ ] I wouldn't play.

4 Imagine you had $150 to buy a new bike, but your best friend called you and asked if he could borrow $150. What would you do?
- [ ] I'd lend him the money and buy a cheaper bike.
- [ ] I wouldn't give him the money.
- [ ] I'd tell him to talk to his parents about the problem.

5 Imagine you were having dinner at your friend's house and his dad served you some vegetables that you really didn't like. What would you do?
- [ ] I'd tell him that I didn't like them.
- [ ] I'd leave them on my plate.
- [ ] I'd hide them in my pockets.

A Song 4 U If I were you

 17

(4) Listen and complete the song using the words on the left.

sad
would
were
goodbye (x2)
weren't
road
had
wheel

Chorus:
Turn the ¹............. back
Go and try
It won't work
I tell you ².............
Turn the wheel back
Go and try
Everyone has got to say
Goodbye.
Oh my dear, if I ³............. you
Then I wouldn't feel all blue,
Then I wouldn't feel all ⁴............. ,
And I wouldn't feel so bad.

Chorus
If I ⁵............. another day,
I would surely like to stay.
If I had another year,
I ⁶............. surely spend it here.
Chorus
If my life ⁷............. all mapped out,
If I had some little doubt
Where my ⁸............. is leading to,
I would surely stay with you.
Chorus
Oh my dear, if I were you,
Then I wouldn't feel all blue.
Life goes on, we wave ⁹............. ,
Meet again maybe some day.

Writing for your Portfolio

(5) Write dilemma questions with three answers. Put all the dilemmas together and make a class questionnaire. Compare your answers.

> *Example:*
> *Imagine you borrowed a CD from a friend and you lost it.*
> *What would you do?*
> *I would buy another one.*
> *I would hope he / she forgot about it.*
> *I would say I was sorry.*

MORE fun with Fido

Now, here's a dilemma. There's some delicious meat in the cat's bowl...

But, of course, it's for the cat and not for me. Now, should I eat it or leave it?

Not a difficult dilemma to solve.

Number challenges

Key words

divide by	subtract	sum (or total)	row	horizontal
multiply by	a half	digit	column	vertical
add (up)	circular	square	diagonal	

18 **1** **Work in pairs. Try to find the answers to these questions. Take notes. Then listen and check.**

a   What's 50 divided by a half?

b   If there are three pizzas and you take away two, how many do you have?

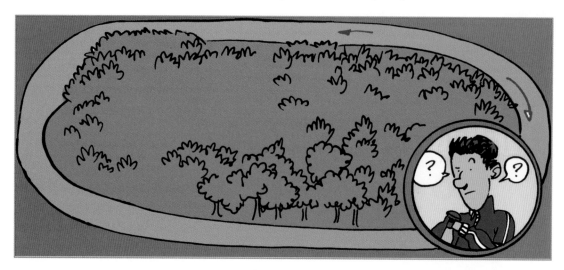

c   A man lives next to a circular park. In the park, there are exactly 356 trees. Every morning, the man walks around the park. It takes him 80 minutes to walk around the park in a clockwise direction, but 1 hour 20 minutes to walk around it in a counterclockwise direction. Why?

d   You are driving a train from New York City to Philadelphia. The train leaves at 11:00 and travels for two hours. There is a 20-minute stop in Newark and a half hour stop in East Brunswick. Then the train continues for another three hours. What's the driver's name?

e   Three friends have a meal at a restaurant. The check is $30, so each of them pays $10. Ten minutes later (the friends are still in the restaurant) the waiter notices a mistake on the check. He charged $5 too much. So he takes five one-dollar bills from the till to give to the three friends. On his way to their table, the waiter decides to keep $2 as a tip because it is difficult to divide $5 by 3. He gives each of the friends $1 back. So each of the friends paid $9. The waiter kept $2, so the total is $29. What happened to the missing $1?

2 **Practice this magic number trick yourself first. Then show it to a friend.**

1 On a piece of paper, write the number NINE (in words). Do not show it to your friend. Fold the paper and put it in an envelope. Seal the envelope and give it to your friend. Ask him/her not to open it yet.

2 Tell your friend to take a piece of paper and write down the last two digits of their phone number. Tell them to add the number of dollars (or yen, yuan, euros, pesos, or whatever the currency in your country is) they have in their pocket to the last two numbers of their phone number.

3 Tell your friend to add his/her age and the number of their house or apartment.

4 Tell them to subtract the number of brothers and sisters they have.

5 Tell them to subtract 12. Then add their favorite number.

6 Your friend should now multiply the total by 18.

7 Tell your friend to add up all the digits in the final total.

8 If the answer is more than 1 digit long, your friend should add up the digits again. (If necessary, your friend should do this until there is only one digit left).

9 Tell your friend that you know exactly what the answer is. Ask them to open the envelope and check.

Mini-project Make a magic square for someone's birthday

1 If you are looking for a nice birthday present for someone, you can easily create a magic square for them. The person must be older than 22. Lisa made this card for her mother, who is 37. Add up the numbers in every row and in every column. Then check the diagonal lines in the middle. Find out if Lisa got it right.

8	11	17	1
16	2	7	12
3	19	9	6
10	5	4	18

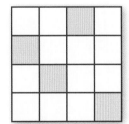

2 Can you create a magic square for someone? Remember, though, the person has to be over 22 years old.

3 To check and find out how you can do this, listen and take notes.

1 Oliver is going to Botswana with his parents. Read the emails he writes to his friend Sam back home.

Hi Sam,

I'm going to spend my summer vacation this year in Botswana with my parents. "Where's that?" you'll ask. I'll tell you in a minute because I've checked it out. The story is that Mom and Dad are going to Botswana to show people how to use the water they have in a better way. Yesterday, they told me that I'm coming, too. They have already had all their equipment flown out to Botswana. We're going next week, can you imagine? I'm pretty excited. It must be amazing there. I still have a lot to do though. Later today, I'm going to have my passport photo taken! #:-O)

See you,

Oliver

Botswana. Facts for my friends:

It's not in South Africa, it's in Africa just north of South Africa in fact. It's almost as big as the state of Texas. Any idea how many people live there? Well, I'll tell you: there are only one-and-a-half million people! Imagine that. There can't be a lot of towns and cities. As big as Texas, but only 1.5 million people. There are about 25 million in Texas. Most of Botswana is desert, so water must be a very important thing. And the official language is English! Most people speak English and Setswana. So, that's enough for now. Look at the map. Check out where Gabarone is. That's the capital. It's where we're going to fly first.

In this unit

You learn
- to make deductions
- causative *have*
- infinitives of purpose
- words for vacations

and then you can
- give reasons
- talk about vacation plans
- make deductions

2 **Answer the questions below.**

1 Why are Oliver and his family going to Botswana?
2 What does Oliver have to do before he goes to Botswana?
3 How does Botswana compare to the state of Texas (size and number of people)?
4 Why is water so important to people in Botswana?
5 What language(s) do people in Botswana speak?
6 What is the capital of Botswana?

Get talking Giving reasons

20 **3** **Listen and repeat.**

A Where do you want to go on vacation this year?
B I want to go to Africa.
A Why?
B To go on safari.

A Are you going on vacation this year?
B Yes, we want to go to Mexico.
A Why?
B To relax on a beach.

21 **4** **Match the pictures with the activities. Then listen and check.**

1 go on safari	4 go mountain climbing	7 go skiing
2 go surfing	5 see the Statue of Liberty	8 relax on a beach
3 go camping	6 go hiking	9 go horseback riding

 A
 B
 C
 D
 E
 F
 G
 H
 I

5 **Check the activities you want to do on vacation and decide which of the places below is the best place to do them. Work with a partner and make up similar dialogues to those in Exercise 3.**

Africa   Mexico   Canada   Australia   Japan   the U.S.

Language Focus

Vocabulary Vacation words

22 **1** **Listen and complete the phrases using the words on the left.**

book
buy
look at
make
find out
rent
check out
take

1 .... a flight
2 .... a trip
3 .... a hotel reservation
4 .... a car
5 .... a map of the area
6 .... the area .... on the web
7 .... what to do there
8 .... a dictionary

2 **Work with a partner. Student A: Close your book. Student B: Ask four questions to see how many verbs Student A can remember from Exercise 1. Switch roles.**

B make a hotel reservation

A What's number 3?

Get talking Talking about vacation plans

23 **3** **Listen and complete the dialogue with the correct words.**

surfing
booked
vacation
made
camping

A Where are you going on [1] .... this year?
B We're going camping near the coast. I'm going to learn [2] ....
and windsurfing.
A Cool! Have you [3] .... a flight?
B Yes, we have.
A Have you [4] .... a hotel reservation?
B No, we haven't. It's a [5] .... trip!

Sounds right Question intonation

24 **4** **Listen and repeat.**

A Do you have any plans for your vacation?
B Yes, I have.

A Have you booked your flight yet?
B No, I haven't.

5 **Work with a partner. Talk about your vacation plans. Use the language below.**

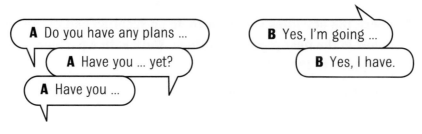

A Do you have any plans ...

A Have you ... yet?

A Have you ...

B Yes, I'm going ...

B Yes, I have.

Grammar

Making deductions

1 **Complete the sentences with one word. Then check against the text on page 94.**

I'm pretty excited. It ¹ .... be amazing there.
There are only one-and-a-half million people! Imagine that. There ² .... be a lot of towns and cities.

When you make an affirmative deduction, use *must*:
He won the game. He **must be** happy. (I'm sure that he <u>is</u> happy.)

When you make a negative deduction, use *can't*:
He lost the game. He **can't be** happy. (I'm sure that he <u>is not</u> happy.)

2 **Circle the correct option.**

1   She has 30 birthday cards. She *must / can't* have a lot of friends.
2   He's calling from a pay phone. His cell phone *must / can't* be broken.
3   She doesn't speak Spanish. She *must / can't* be from Peru.
4   She looks young. She *must / can't* be more than 20.
5   He's got hundreds of CDs. He *must / can't* love music.
6   He didn't eat anything. He *must / can't* like pizza very much.

3 **Write deductions about these people. Use the words below to help you.**

1 happy   2 old enough   3 very   4 hungry   5 Italian
He must   ....   intelligent   ....
be happy   ....
                                    ....

Get talking Making deductions

4 **Work in pairs. Student A: Choose sentences from column A. Student B: Choose a suitable answer from column B. Switch roles.**

A	B
I haven't eaten for six hours.	You've already eaten two. You can't be hungry.
I have lost the CDs I bought yesterday.	You must be hungry.
Linda told me she's broken my MP3 player.	You must be angry.
I'd like another burger.	You must be sad.
Can you get me another sweater, please?	You've already got three. You can't be cold.

Causative *have*

(5) **Put the words in the correct order. Then check against the text on page 94.**

I'm going / passport photo / to / taken / have / my

They / flown out / had / their equipment / have / to Botswana

We use this structure to say that another person does/did the action for us.

I had my photo **taken** last week. (= I did not take it myself, another person took it)

Form: Person + (form of the verb *have*) + object + past participle of the main verb.

(6) **Complete the phrases with one of the verbs on the right.**

1 to have your hair ....

2 to have your room ....

3 to have your hair ....

4 to have your bike ....

5 to have a window ....

6 to have a carpet ....

cut
painted
fixed (2)
changed
dyed

(7) **Look at the pictures and talk about what David and Hannah have had done.**

He's had his hair cut.

....

She's had her room painted.

....

Infinitives of purpose

(8) **Join the sentences together. Use *to* and *because*.**

1 Mary bought a new dress. She wants to wear it to the party.
   Mary bought a new dress to wear to the party.
   Mary bought a new dress because she wants to wear it to the party.

2 John called me. He wanted to invite me to the party.
   ....
   ....

3 Ben bought a new bike. He wanted to get some exercise.
   ....
   ....

4 I went to the newsstand. I wanted to get the new *City Review* magazine.
   ....
   ....

5 Jill turned off the TV. She wanted to read a book.
   ....
   ....

Skills

Reading

1 Find out what happened to Oliver on his trip.

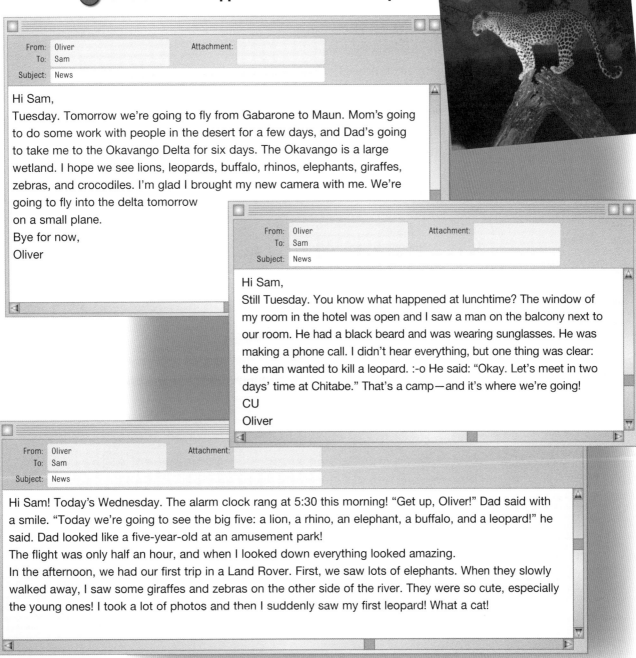

From: Oliver
To: Sam
Attachment:
Subject: News

Hi Sam,
Tuesday. Tomorrow we're going to fly from Gabarone to Maun. Mom's going to do some work with people in the desert for a few days, and Dad's going to take me to the Okavango Delta for six days. The Okavango is a large wetland. I hope we see lions, leopards, buffalo, rhinos, elephants, giraffes, zebras, and crocodiles. I'm glad I brought my new camera with me. We're going to fly into the delta tomorrow on a small plane.
Bye for now,
Oliver

From: Oliver
To: Sam
Attachment:
Subject: News

Hi Sam,
Still Tuesday. You know what happened at lunchtime? The window of my room in the hotel was open and I saw a man on the balcony next to our room. He had a black beard and was wearing sunglasses. He was making a phone call. I didn't hear everything, but one thing was clear: the man wanted to kill a leopard. :-o He said: "Okay. Let's meet in two days' time at Chitabe." That's a camp—and it's where we're going!
CU
Oliver

From: Oliver
To: Sam
Attachment:
Subject: News

Hi Sam! Today's Wednesday. The alarm clock rang at 5:30 this morning! "Get up, Oliver!" Dad said with a smile. "Today we're going to see the big five: a lion, a rhino, an elephant, a buffalo, and a leopard!" he said. Dad looked like a five-year-old at an amusement park!
The flight was only half an hour, and when I looked down everything looked amazing.
In the afternoon, we had our first trip in a Land Rover. First, we saw lots of elephants. When they slowly walked away, I saw some giraffes and zebras on the other side of the river. They were so cute, especially the young ones! I took a lot of photos and then I suddenly saw my first leopard! What a cat!

2 Read the text in Exercise 1 again. Then answer the questions.

1 What is the Okavango Delta? ....

2 Which animals did Oliver hope to see in the delta? ....

3 What did Oliver hear in the hotel at lunchtime? ....

4 What did the man look like? ....

5 How long did the flight into the delta take? ....

6 What animals did Oliver see on his first trip into the delta? ....

Listening

 Listen to Sam talking about Oliver's emails. Then complete the sentences.

broken arm / man had a cut on his head	arrested the two men	landed on its roof	control
the hotel / wanted to kill the leopard	the life of a leopard	~~wanted to kill a leopard~~	
wanted to come to their camp	a black car	the car before	

1 Oliver told Alex, the driver, about a man who ..*wanted to kill a leopard*..

2 Oliver told Alex that the man ....

3 On the afternoon drive Alex suddenly saw ....

4 The other guide had never seen ....

5 The driver of the black car lost ....

6 The black car rolled over and ....

7 One man had a ...., and the other

....

8 The man with the broken arm was the man from ....

who ....

9 The park rangers ....

10 Alex said that Oliver had saved ....

Writing for your Portfolio

4 Read the summary of part of Oliver's adventures in Botswana. Check it against the text on page 99. Find and correct three mistakes.

> On Thursday Oliver went to camp Chitabe in the Okavango Delta with his dad to see the animals. The day before they went, Oliver heard three men talking about killing an elephant at the camp. He was worried. At the delta they saw lots of amazing animals, including a leopard.

5 Look at the script of the story. Write a summary of what happened next. Don't write more than 50 words.

Writing tips Summary writing

- Look at the text and underline the <u>important</u> information. This is the information that you really need to retell the story.
- Think about ways that you can make this information shorter. What words can you leave out?
- Rewrite the sentences. Don't use the sentences from the text.
- When you have finished, read your summary again to make sure that it is clear and easy to understand.

Check your progress Units 9 and 10

1 **Reorder the letters and write words for parts of the computer.**

1 semou ....
2 medom ....
3 nterpri ....
4 krsespea ....
5 boyekrda .... ☐ **5**

2 **Complete the phrases.**

1 book a f _ _ _ _ _
2 plan a t _ _ _
3 make a r _ _ _ _ _ _ _ _ _ _
4 look at a m _ _
5 buy a d _ _ _ _ _ _ _ _ ☐ **5**

3 **Complete the dialogue with** *everyone*, *someone*, *no one*, **and** *anyone*.

A ¹........... knows Marco. He's very popular.
B When I arrived at this school last year. I didn't know ².............. . Marco was the first person I spoke to.
A ³........... likes their first day at school.
B It was terrible. I really needed ⁴.............. to talk to and I found Marco! ☐ **4**

4 **Complete using the second conditional.**

1 I .... (go) if I ....(know) the address.
2 If they .... (have) more money, they .... (buy) the house.
3 If she ....(get) a job, she .... (be) happier.
4 We .... (help) them if they .... (need) it.
5 He ...... (learn) more English if he .... (go) to New York.
6 If they .... (speak) more clearly, we .... (understand) them. ☐ **6**

5 **Complete the sentences with a verb and the causative** *have*.

1 He .... his hair .... (cut) yesterday.
2 We .... our photos .... (take) there.
3 She .... her bag ....(steal)
4 They .... their car .... (check) today.
5 I always .... my papers .... (deliver)
6 She .... her bike .... (fix) yesterday. ☐ **6**

6 **Write advice using** *If I were you,...* **and the verbs below.**

1 .... (do a paper route)
2 .... (go out more)
3 .... (go running) ☐ **6**

7 **Write a deduction for each sentence.**

1 I haven't had lunch. (hungry)
....
2 I've just passed my exams. (happy)
....
3 He's just lost his job. (upset)
....
4 She's just opened the window. (hot)
....
5 You slept until 1:00 p.m. (tired)
.... ☐ **10**

8 **Complete the sentences using** *to* **or** *because*.

1 My dad lent me money .... I want to buy a car.
2 I went to the library .... I wanted a book.
3 He turned off the TV .... he needed to work.
4 My friend called .... invite me to the movies. ☐ **8**

TOTAL ☐ **50**

My progress so far is ...

☺ 😐 ☹
great! ☐ good. ☐ poor. ☐

Volunteer vacation

1 **Read about *summer volunteer programs for teens.*
Then answer the questions.**

It is becoming more and more common for teenagers to spend their summer vacation helping other people.

Landmark Volunteers is one organization that helps teenagers find the right volunteer vacation for them. It gives high-school students aged 14 and a half and older opportunities to build homes, clear and restore nature trails, help children with disabilities, and much more.

Most of the programs run for one or two weeks. Teenagers can choose to go on one of 63 programs all around North America. They work as part of a team with a group of 12 other high-school students from around the country.

Do you know?

During the summer, many American students choose to travel or do volunteer work. Sometimes students join a program such as Landmark Volunteers, or BUNAC.

1 What is the name of the organization that can help teens find a volunteer vacation?
2 How long are the summer programs?
3 How old do you have to be to volunteer?
4 What are some of the things volunteers can do?

26 **2** **Listen and write the name of the correct organization under each photo.**

Global Works Travel   Landmark Volunteers   BUNAC

Organization:
....

Organization:
....

Organization:
....

3 **Over 2 U!** **What would you do if you had the opportunity?
Interview your classmates and write down who would do what.**

Would you like to ...?
Yes, I would. No, I wouldn't. I would like to ...

MORE! Now you can watch Episode 5 of *The School Magazine!*

THE LEOPARD THAT LOST ITS SPOTS

If you count a leopard's spots
You'll find that it's got lots and lots.
(Only other leopards know
Just how many spots they grow.)

Lenny was a leopard small
Who one day heard his mother call:
"Lenny's sick! What has he got?
He's lost his biggest, blackest spot!"
Poor Lenny hunted high and low,
Just where it was he didn't know.
The other leopards looked around,
But still the spot could not be found.

Now in the jungle lived a man,
And down to him young Lenny ran.
He told him of his missing spot.
The man said, "I know what I've got!"
He went into his grassy den
And came out with a little pen.

Soon Lenny ran back home again,
His visit had not been in vain.
Upon his back, what do you think?
A brand new spot in thick, black ink!
The leopards thanked the man who plotted
To make their Lenny fully spotted!

For **MORE!** Go to www.cambridge.org/elt/americanmore and take a quiz on this text.

In this unit

You learn

- reported speech 1
- *want/ask/tell* someone to do something
- words for the environment

and then you can

- say what you want people to do

27 **1** **Read and listen to the dialogue.**

Karen Did you hear about the park?

Claire No. What about it?

Karen They say that they want to cut down some of the trees and make it much smaller. They want to build a car park and they need part of the park for the entrance, the part near South Street.

Claire But that means we can't play there any more. What can I do to help?

Karen I want you to go and talk to other people in the park. Then we can decide on a plan of action.

(*The next day*)

Karen Oliver and I went to the city council yesterday and talked to an official there. He told us they are going to do it. He told us not to worry. He said that we'll still have half the park to play in!

Claire That's true, but there's no playing field in the other half.

Karen I know! Work's going to start in a month. He asked us to support the city council. But I want to organize a protest march through the park.

Rick What about a petition? We can ask people to sign it!

Karen Good idea!

2 **Match the sentence halves.**

1 Karen says that they want to cut down
2 She says that they want to build
3 Karen says that she
4 Oliver and Karen go to the city council
5 The city planner wants them to
6 They want to write a petition,

a wants Claire to talk to other people in the park.
b and speak to a city planner there.
c trees and make the park smaller.
d support the city council.
e and organize a protest march.
f a car park.

Get talking Saying what you want people to do

28 **3** **Listen and repeat.**

A I want you to do something for me.
B What is it?
A I want you to mail a letter.
B OK, I'll do that right away.

A I want you to do something for me.
B What is it?
A I want you to come to the grocery store with me.
B I'm sorry, I can't. I have to do my homework.

29 **4** **Match the phrases with the pictures. Listen and check.**

1 do the dishes
4 mail a letter

2 buy me an ice-cream cone
5 go grocery shopping

3 help me with my homework
6 lend me some money

5 **Work with a partner. Make dialogues like the ones from Exercise 3. Use ideas in the pictures above.**

Language Focus

Vocabulary The environment

1 Match the phrases and the pictures.

HOW GREEN ARE YOU?

A **1** Save water.

B Don't take plastic bags to your supermarket. **BRING A BASKET.**

C Ride your **bike** or **walk**.

D Recycle glass bottles.

E DON'T BE A LITTERBUG

F RECYCLE PAPER.

2 Read the questionnaire and circle your answers. See how "green" you are.

What's your green score?

1 I (a) always (b) sometimes (c) hardly ever (d) never save water.

2 I (a) always (b) sometimes (c) hardly ever (d) never recycle glass jars.

3 I (a) never (b) hardly ever (c) sometimes (d) always throw paper and plastic bottles on the ground.

4 When leaving the beach I (a) never (b) hardly ever (c) sometimes (d) always leave litter behind.

5 I (a) always (b) sometimes (c) hardly ever (d) never put paper into special containers to be recycled.

6 I (a) always (b) sometimes (c) hardly ever (d) never ask my parents to drive me short distances.

Scores

If you circled (a) at least four times: You are very "green."

If you circled (b) at least four times: You are mostly "green." Keep it up.

If you circled (c) at least four times: You probably know what you should do, but you are too lazy.

If you circled (d) at least four times: You are a litterbug. You are not "green" at all.

Grammar

Reported speech 1

1 **Look at the dialogue on page 104 and complete the examples.**

He ¹ .... are going to do it.
He ² ....'ll still have half the park to play in.

2 **Complete the rule with *say* or *tell*.**

When we report what people say, we often use the verbs *say* and *tell*.
¹ .... is not followed by an object.
² .... is followed by an object.

Make sure you change the pronoun.
Helen said, "**You** look sad." = She said that **I** look sad.
Bob said, "**We** might be late." = He said **they** might be late.
Trevor said, "It's **my** birthday." = He told us that it's **his** birthday.

3 **Circle the correct option.**

1 He *says / says me* that he doesn't speak English very well.
2 They *told / told us* they were Spanish.
3 She *told / told her* she wasn't coming.
4 He *says / says him* he wants more French fries.

4 **Complete the sentences.**

1 "I'm hungry," says Paul.
  Paul says that .he.is.hungry..
2 "We're going home," Jenny tells me.
  Jenny tells me ...
3 "I'm not happy," says Sue.
  Sue ...
4 "You look like my sister," the girl tells me.
  The girl ...
5 "You are tired!" she tells us.
  She ...
6 "They are going to sell the house," May says. May ...

want / ask / tell someone to do something

We often use the verb *want* with an object pronoun + *to*.

I want **you** to go and talk to other people in the park.
I **don't** want **you** to tell anyone.

The verbs *ask* and *tell* have a similar construction in the negative form. Note the position of *not*.
He told us **not to** worry.
He **asked** me **not to** tell anyone.

5 **Match the sentences and pictures.**

1 He wants you to take him for a walk.
2 I want you to go to sleep now.
3 He asked me to marry him.
4 She asked me not to drive so fast.
5 She told him not to run.
6 He told me to be quiet.

6 Put the words in order to make sentences.

1 help / he / to / him / asked / me   *He asked me to help him.*
2 buy / she / to / some / him / milk / asked   ....
3 say / they / not / me / to / anything / asked   ....
4 I / for / her / to / told / me / wait   ....
5 not / we / them / to / anything / touch / told   ....
6 with / he / wanted / to / me / him / go   ....

7 Make the sentences negative.

1 I want you to turn off the TV.   *I don't want you to turn off the TV.*
2 He told me to leave.   ....
3 We asked them to be there at 5:00 p.m.   ....
4 She told us to buy some bread.   ....
5 Dave wants us to arrive early.   ....
6 I told them to play in the yard.   ....

30

8 Complete the dialogue with the phrases on the right. Listen and check. Then act it out.

Sandra Gerry?
Gerry What is it, Sandra?
Sandra I want you ¹.............................
Gerry What is it?
Sandra ².................... me they are planning to build a highway through our neighborhood.
Gerry Through our neighborhood? No way!
Sandra Exactly. ³............................. work's going to start next month. That's why ⁴............................. to help me.
Gerry Help you with what?
Sandra We want to ⁵............................. a petition and ⁶............................. leaflets to all the people in the neighborhood.
Gerry That's a great idea.
Sandra Will you help us?
Gerry Of course.

Someone told
write
give
I want you
She said
to do something
for me

9 Choose one of the situations below and write a short dialogue like the one in Exercise 8. Then act it out.

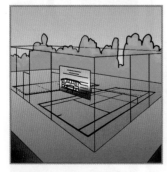

There are plans to build a supermarket where the tennis courts are.

Children are not allowed to use school computers unless a teacher is in the room.

The school library is not open in the afternoon anymore.

They want to fill in the pond in the park to make room for a parking lot.

Skills

Reading and writing

1 Read about how these people made a difference and answer the questions below.

ECONOMY and ECOLOGY

Those who speak up can make a difference.

Wangari Maathai. Wangari Maathai (b. 1940) from Kenya won the Nobel Peace Prize in 2004 for her fight for democracy and for the environment. She was the first African woman to win the prize. Maathai founded the Green Belt Movement in Kenya in 1977, which has planted more than 10 million trees. But she went to jail many times because of her fight for the rights of women and because of her work for the environment. In 2002, she won a seat in the Kenyan parliament.

Erin Brockovich. In the early 1990s, Erin Brockovich (b. 1960), a single mother of three, was working for a law firm. While sorting out papers one day, she discovered that many people who lived in and around Hinkley, California, in the 1960s–1980s were very sick. She later found out that there was poison in the water. It came from a gas and electricity company. In 1996, she and lawyer Ed Masry won $333 million for more than 600 people from Hinkley.

Al Gore In 2007, former U.S. vice president Al Gore won a surprising award. It was surprising because what he won was an Oscar, an award normally given to movie stars! He won the Oscar for his 2006 movie, called *An Inconvenient Truth*. This movie tells people about global warming. Since 2000, Al Gore has told millions of people about the effects of global warming. He has also won many awards for his work.

---

1 What does the Green Belt Movement in Kenya do?

2 Who won the Nobel Peace Prize in 2004?

3 What did Erin Brockovich discover about Hinkley, California?

4 Which "surprising" award did Al Gore win?

5 How many people did Erin Brockovich help win money for?

2 Summarize what each person did in one sentence.

Listening

 3 **Listen to these students talking about their favorite hero/heroine. Complete the table.**

	Hannah	John	Natasha
Who?	Mahatma Gandhi		
Why?			

Speaking

4 **In pairs, talk about your heroes. Then tell the class.**

One of my heroes is ....
I admire him/her because ....
I think it is/was really great, the way she/he ....
I think it's great that she/he ....
She/he usually ....
Once she/he ....
I admire how much .... she/he has.

Writing for your Portfolio

5 **Design a leaflet for something you want to stand up for.**

Make sure you:
- have a good slogan
- say what it is all about
- say what you are planning to do

MAKE RIDING BIKES SAFE!
Say **yes** to a
new bike path!!
Ride to the next meeting and join our
PROTEST RIDE
to the Town Hall!
Saturday, 3:00 p.m.
in front of the school!

Keep on riding!

A Song 4 U We shall overcome

32

6 **Can you name either of the people in the photos? Listen to the song.**

We shall overcome,
We shall overcome,
We shall overcome some day.

Chorus:
Oh deep in my heart,
I do believe,
We shall overcome some day.

We'll walk hand in hand,
We'll walk hand in hand,
We'll walk hand in hand some day.

Chorus

We shall all be free,
We shall all be free,
We shall all be free some day.

Chorus

We are not afraid,
We are not afraid,
We are not afraid today.

Chorus

We are not alone,
We are not alone,
We are not alone today.

Chorus

The whole wide world around,
The whole wide world around,
The whole wide world around some day.

Chorus

We shall overcome,
We shall overcome,
We shall overcome some day.

Chorus

Energy and how to save it

Key words

energy consumption   heat   gas pump   renewable energy
(energy-saving) lightbulb   blackout   photovoltaic (PV) cells   (marine) current
average temperature   increase   wind turbine   source (of energy)
(powering and lighting)   tide   insulation
   appliances

1   **Energy consumption. Read the text.**

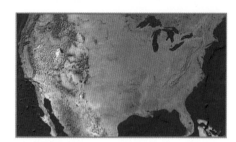

If you look at North America from space at night, you can see how developed countries light up the world.

Imagine the following situation. It's nine o'clock at night in New York City. Suddenly, there is a blackout in the eastern states of the U.S. Subway trains come to a halt. TV screens go blank, washing machines stop, everything is dark. Blackouts happen because more and more people use more and more energy. In the last 40 years, energy consumption has increased by 250 percent. Scientists think that by the year 2030, energy use will have doubled. And that will cause great problems.

33

2   **How do we use energy at home?**
Guess what people in North America used energy for in 2005. Then listen and check.

1	air-conditioning	About 41%
2	lighting and powering appliances	About 20%
3	heating water	About 26%
4	heating rooms in the house	About 8%

3   **Space heating.**

The picture on the right shows how energy is lost. In the picture, energy is lost through the windows, roofs, and walls.

Look at the average temperatures in homes since 1970. What was the increase—20%, 35%, or 50%?

1970	12.6°C
1990	16.9°C
2001	18.9°C

4 **Energy alternatives and saving energy. Read the text.**

Photovoltaic (PV) cells on roof shingles take the sun's energy and generate electricity. Especially in hot countries, solar power will become one of the most important sources of renewable energy in the future.

Energy-saving lightbulbs use only a fifth of what traditional bulbs use.

Insulation helps reduce the energy consumption of old houses. When a new house is built, the temperature in the house is higher if the house faces south and if there is a lot of glass that catches the sun.

Wind turbines produce renewable energy, but there is a problem. There have been protests because some people think that they make beautiful landscapes look ugly.

There are currents in the ocean because of the tides. When we use underwater turbines (in much the same way that a wind turbine works), we can make electricity. The advantage is that this form of energy is always there. Work is going on to develop marine current turbines. These could be built in groups under the ocean, like an underwater wind farm.

Think about how you get to school. Many students are driven to school by their parents. You can save energy if you walk or ride your bike to school.

Mini-project Saving energy

5 Check the Internet or a library for facts about how you can save energy. Design a leaflet, including facts, advice, and illustrations about how to save energy at home or in school.

1 Read about California.

California

Here we come!

"We are in the Joshua Tree National Park in the desert. It's amazing! The shapes of the trees are just incredible. Some look like strange animals!"

"We are in Universal Studios today! It's so cool! There's an earthquake experience and you get attacked by the shark from *Jaws*! We also want to go to the Walk of Fame, where lots of famous actors have a pink star on the sidewalk!"

California
STATE OF CONTRASTS!

by Steven Doyle

Last month, I decided to visit and experience California, one of the most popular and famous states in the U.S. At my hotel, I met David and Emma from the state of Ohio. I asked them why they were here. They said they were on vacation there with their parents, and they told me they were going to the Joshua Tree National Park that day. I saw them later in the evening. They said that the park was amazing. I wanted to know if they planned to visit again.

They said they wanted to as there were still so many things to see like Yosemite National Park and San Francisco.

That's the thing about California. It's landscape is diverse, with mountains, deserts, and famous places. Of course, its main attraction must be Hollywood. Thousands of people go there every year to visit the Walk of Fame in Los Angeles and to experience their favorite movies at Universal Studios. I met Jane and Sarah at the hotel who told me their visit to Universal Studios was one of the best days of their lives! So if you want to go to a great place with many different things to see and do, visit the "Sunshine State" of California!

In this unit

You learn
- reported speech 2
- words for physical appearance

and then you can
- justify opinions
- identify a person

2 Circle T (True) or F (False) for the sentences below.

1 California is known as the "Golden State." T / F
2 There are no deserts in California. T / F
3 There is a national park in California. T / F
4 California has a lot of different scenery. T / F
5 There is a movie studio you can visit in California. T / F
6 San Francisco and Ohio are in California. T / F

Get talking Justifying opinions

34 **3** Listen to the sentences and practice saying them.

1 I love American people. They are so friendly.
2 Universal Studios is so cool! It's fun and interesting.

35 **4** Match the sentences. Listen and check. Then practice saying them.

1 The beaches in California are good.
2 The mountains in Yosemite National Park are amazing.
3 San Francisco is great.
4 California is a friendly place.
5 Santa Cruz is a cool city on the coast.

a It's a hilly city and there's always something to do there.
b There's always a big welcome there for you.
c They're really clean and sandy.
d It has some great beaches.
e They're so high.

5 Make a list of countries and cities you have been to or heard about. Tell a partner about them and justify your opinions.

> London is a bit boring.
> It's always raining there.

> New York City is an exciting city.
> There's a lot of things to do there.

Language Focus

Vocabulary Physical appearance

hair
body
~~eyes~~
clothes
hair

36

1 **Complete the lists with the words on the left. Listen and check.**

1 gray / blue / brown / green ......*eyes*..........
2 curly / straight / short / long / thin ....
3 tall / short / thin / slim / well-built / muscular ....
4 casual / elegant / shabby / dressy / dirty / sporty ....
5 blonde / red / gray / brown / white / black / dyed ....

Get talking Identifying a person

2 **Work in pairs. Choose a person in the picture. Describe what he or she looks like. Your partner points to the correct person in the picture.**

A I'm thinking of a boy. He has red curly hair, his clothes are casual, and he's short and muscular. Who is he?

B This boy here.

Grammar

Reported speech 2

(1) **Complete the sentences. Then check against the text on page 114.**

1 "We want to visit again." → They .... they .... to visit again.
2 "Why are you here?" → I asked them .... they .... here.
3 "Do you plan to visit again?" → I wanted to know .... they .... to visit again.

- When we report someone's words, we often change the verb tense (see sentences 1, 2, and 3).
- When we report a question, we use the same question word (*who/what/why*, etc.) (see sentence 2).
- When we report a *Yes/No* question, we use the word *if* (see sentence 3).
- When we report questions, we <u>don't</u> use *do/does/did* or the question word order (see sentences 2 and 3).

(2) **Circle the correct form of the verb.**

1 Joanne says that she *likes / liked* traveling.
2 Barbara told me that she *is going / was going* to Australia on vacation
3 Our friends said that they *are staying / were staying* at a nice hotel.
4 He said he *doesn't like / didn't like* the beaches in Santa Monica.
5 I said I *am / was* very happy.
6 They tell us that they *love / loved* the sun.
7 She says that she *has / had* no time.
8 You told me you *write / wrote* 10 emails every day.

(3) **Present or past? Complete the sentences with the correct form of the verb.**

1 She told me that her uncle .... on a farm. (live)
2 She says she .... ice cream. (not like)
3 They told us that the weather .... great. (be)
4 Tony says he .... very happy about this. (be)
5 He says he never .... DVDs at home. (watch)

6 They told us that they .... in San Diego. (be)
7 Caroline said that she .... Carl. (love)

(4) **Complete the sentences. Choose the correct question word.**

where	~~why~~	how much	if (x3)

1 She said, "Why are you angry?"
   She wanted to know ....*why*..... I was angry.
2 He said, "Do you watch a lot of TV?"
   He asked her .... she watched a lot of TV.
3 They asked me, "Are you a student?"
   They wanted to know .... I was a student.
4 She asked, "Where's your brother?"
   She asked .... my brother was.
5 He said, "Do you like sports?"
   He asked .... I liked sports.
6 She asked, "How much are the pink jeans?"
   She asked me .... the pink jeans were.

Game

(5) Work in groups of four. Each member of the group needs four strips of paper. Write a different sentence about yourself on each strip of paper. Add your first name. Two of the sentences should be true and two must be false. All four sentences should be in the present tense. Hand out your strips of paper to the other members of the group.

Sue said that she had two cats. I think that's true.

Yes, it's true.

Meg said that she was going to Shanghai on vacation. I think that's false.

No, it's not false, it's true.

Luke said that his father drives a Ford. I think that's true.

No, it's not true, it's false.

Mark said that he liked science best of all subjects. I think that's false.

Yes, it's false.

Sounds right Word stress

37

(6) Listen to the stress in these words, and then write them in the correct column. Listen again and check.

A ☐☐☐☐   B ☐☐☐☐

....
....
....
....

....
....
....
....

politician
information
education
incredible
photographer
European
American
identify

38

(7) Listen and repeat.

1 He's an American photographer.
2 I had an incredible education.
3 She's a European politician.
4 I can't identify the information.

Skills

Reading

1 **Read the texts. Put the phrases A–D in the correct places.**

A This is a place where

B the stars aren't only human

C Don't forget to go on

D a little more contemporary

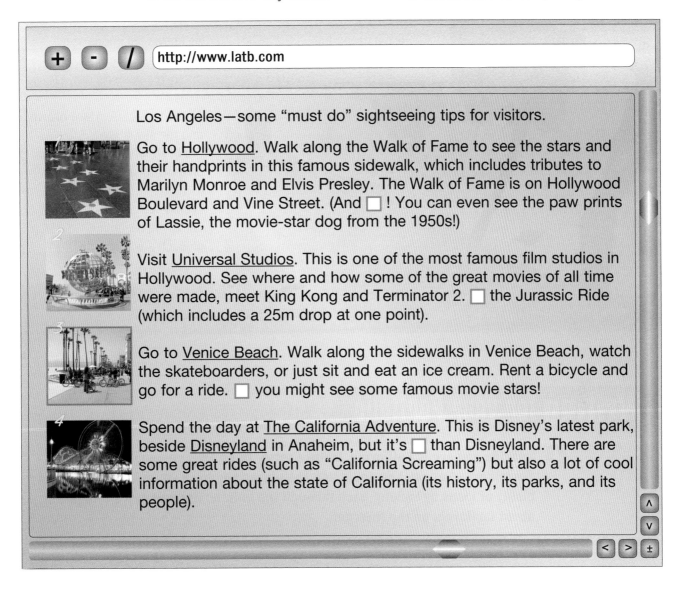

http://www.latb.com

Los Angeles—some "must do" sightseeing tips for visitors.

Go to <u>Hollywood</u>. Walk along the Walk of Fame to see the stars and their handprints in this famous sidewalk, which includes tributes to Marilyn Monroe and Elvis Presley. The Walk of Fame is on Hollywood Boulevard and Vine Street. (And ☐ ! You can even see the paw prints of Lassie, the movie-star dog from the 1950s!)

Visit <u>Universal Studios</u>. This is one of the most famous film studios in Hollywood. See where and how some of the great movies of all time were made, meet King Kong and Terminator 2. ☐ the Jurassic Ride (which includes a 25m drop at one point).

Go to <u>Venice Beach</u>. Walk along the sidewalks in Venice Beach, watch the skateboarders, or just sit and eat an ice cream. Rent a bicycle and go for a ride. ☐ you might see some famous movie stars!

Spend the day at <u>The California Adventure</u>. This is Disney's latest park, beside <u>Disneyland</u> in Anaheim, but it's ☐ than Disneyland. There are some great rides (such as "California Screaming") but also a lot of cool information about the state of California (its history, its parks, and its people).

Speaking

2 **Imagine you have just come back from Los Angeles. Work with a partner. Interview each other about what you did.**

1 Where did you go?

2 How long did you stay?

3 Did you have a good time?

4 Did you meet any interesting people?

A Song 4 U California dreaming

3 Listen and complete the song with the words on the left.

church   tell
sky   knees
leave   walk
cold   warm
leaves   day

All the leaves are brown,
and the ¹........................ is gray.
I've been for a ²........................
on a winter's day.
I'd be safe and ³........................
if I was in L.A.
California dreaming,
on such a winter's ⁴.........

I stopped into a ⁵........................
I passed along the way.
Well, I got down on my ⁶...............
and I began to pray.
You know, the preacher likes the
⁷........................ ,
he knows I'm gonna stay.
California dreaming,
on such a winter's day.

All the ⁸........................are brown,
and the sky is gray.
I've been for a walk
on a winter's day.
If I didn't ⁹........................ her,
I could ¹⁰........................ today.
California dreaming,
on such a winter's day.

Writing for your Portfolio

4 Imagine you are in California. Write a letter to an English-speaking penpal describing what you are doing and the places you have visited. You will find plenty of ideas by looking back through the unit, or find out more things about California on the Internet.

I am sitting on the beach writing this letter. I can see ...
Yesterday we went to Hollywood, it was ...
On Monday ...
San Francisco is really exciting ...
The best place was ...

Check your progress Units 11 and 12

1 Complete the sentences.

1 Don't be a l _ _ _ _ _ bug.
2 R _ _ _ _ _ _ paper.
3 R _ _ _ your bike.
4 S _ _ _ water.
5 Bring your own b _ _ . `5`

2 Complete the sentences.

1 His hair isn't curly. It's s _ _ _ _ _ _ _ .
2 Her clothes are messy and sh _ _ _ _ .
3 He always wears dr _ _ _ _ suits.
4 She has dy _ _ hair.
5 He exercises a lot and is very mu _ _ _ _ _ _.
6 She isn't tall. She is s _ _ _ _ .
7 She always looks nice and e _ _ _ _ _ _ _ . `7`

3 Write sentences using *want someone to do something*.

1 A: ....
   B: OK. I'll do the dishes.
2 A: ....
   B: OK. Tom will help you with your homework.
3 A: ....
   B: OK. Sue will go grocery shopping. `6`

4 Complete the sentences with the correct pronoun.

1 Mark: "I'm angry." Mark says .... is angry.
2 Rachel: "We're going on vacation tomorrow." Rachel says .... are going on vacation tomorrow.
3 Sue: "You (pl) are hungry!" Sue says .... are hungry.
4 Tom: "They are going to buy a new car." Tom says .... are going to buy a new car. `4`

5 Circle the correct form of the verb.

1 He *told / said* that he didn't like her.
2 They *told / tells* me they were leaving.
3 She *says / tells* that she is happy.
4 He *tells / says* us he is tired. `4`

6 Write the sentences in the negative form.

1 I want you to come tomorrow.
   ....
2 They told me to go.
   ....
3 We asked them to play on the grass.
   ....
4 She told us to go home.
   ....
5 He wants them to leave.
   .... `10`

7 Complete the sentences using indirect speech.

1 She told me her mother .... (be) a teacher.
2 He says he .... (live) near me.
3 They said that they .... (like) ice cream.
4 He tells them he .... (want) some money. `4`

8 Rewrite the sentences using indirect speech.

1 "Do you like pizza?" he asked me.
   ....
2 "Where do you go to school?" she asked him.
   ....
3 "How much money is there?" he asked me.
   ....
4 "Are you a teacher?" they asked her.
   ....
5 "Why are you angry?" he asked them.
   .... `10`

   TOTAL `50`

My progress so far is ...

☺ great! ☐   😐 good. ☐   ☹ poor. ☐

What a waste!

 1 **Listen and then answer the questions about plastic.**

1 What is the problem with plastic?
2 How long will plastic stay in a landfill?
3 Why don't companies want to buy plastic for recycling?
4 What is *Mater-Bi* made of?
5 What is different about *Mater-Bi*?

A lot of the waste produced in the Western world is plastic. Most of the food and drinks we buy in supermarkets are packed in plastic, and in some countries plastic makes up 20 percent of all waste. All of the electronic and electrical appliances we use (such as fridges, cell phones, and laptops) are made of plastic. Plastic is very difficult to get rid of.

2 **Read the text and complete the chart.**

An average cell phone has a lifespan of five years. However, people usually only use a cell phone for about 18 months before they get a new one.

In the U.S., about 130 million cell phones are "retired" each year. That equals about 65,000 tons of electronic garbage. Cell phones contain some dangerous materials. They need to be disposed of in a safe way.

Thankfully, more and more organizations will help you recycle cell phones. Some take your phones for charity. Others may even give you money for a used cell phone.

Phones for recycling
There are some valuable materials in mobile phones such as gold, silver, and copper. The metals are taken out and reused in jewelry, copper pipes, or new cell phones. The plastic can be reused in traffic cones or printer cartridges.

Phones for reuse and repair
Handsets are very expensive and in some countries in Africa and Eastern Europe, people cannot afford them. Phones are sent to these countries and they are given away or resold cheaply.

Research on the Internet to see which cell phone recycling programs are available where you live.

How long do people usually use a cell phone?
1..

How many cell phones are "retired" in the U.S. every year?
2..

How do cell phones need to be disposed of?
3..

How are phones recycled?
4..

What happens to cell phones that are reused?
5..

3 **Over 2 U!** **In pairs, plan a recycling program for your class or school.**

MORE! Now you can watch Episode 6 of *The School Magazine!*

The sound of California

One of the hottest states in the U.S. has also been providing some of the hottest pop and rock music for over half a century. Here are some of the most famous artists from the Sunshine State.

The 1960s

Forget The Beatles and The Rolling Stones! Many critics will tell you that the most influential band in rock history is, in fact, The Beach Boys. The band was started in 1961 in Hawthorne, California, by brothers Brian, Carl, and Denis Wilson, with their cousin Mike Love and friend Alan Jardine.

Their early songs were about being young in California, and talked of things like the sun, beaches, cars (*Fun, Fun, Fun,* and *Little Deuce Coupe*) and surfing (*Surfin' Safari,* and *Surfin' USA*). But as the band got older, their songs became more sophisticated.

During the mid-1960s the band produced their greatest album, *Pet Sounds,* and the single *Good Vibrations*, which is considered by many people as the greatest rock song of all time.

The 1970s

The Eagles were formed in the early 1970s in Los Angeles. Over the next 10 years, they became the best-selling American band of all time with five number one singles and four number one albums. Their *Greatest Hits* album has sold more copies worldwide than any other album except Michael Jackson's *Thriller*.

They are famous for their easy-going, country-style rock made popular by songs such as *Take It Easy, Lying Eyes, Life in the Fast Lane,* and, of course, *Hotel California*.

The band broke up in 1980 but got back together again in 1994 for a series of successful shows around the world. They have also started to record new music to introduce a new generation of fans to the sound of southern California.

The new millennium

In 2006, the Red Hot Chili Peppers showed that they really are the biggest Californian band on the planet when their new CD, *Stadium Arcadium*, went straight into the charts at number one in 27 countries around the world. The band started in 1983 when former Fairfax High School students, Michael "Flea" Balzary (bass), Anthony Kiedis (vocals), Jack Irons (drums), and Hillel Slovak (guitar) got together.

They first played under the name Tony Flow and the Miraculously Majestic Masters of Mayhem. Less than a year later, they were really popular on the Los Angeles rock scene and signed a deal with EMI. Since then, they have released nine studio albums and played to millions of fans all over the world.

With their mixture of alternative rock, punk, rap, funk, and heavy metal, the Red Hot Chili Peppers have created what many people consider to be the sound of modern California.

And the future? These days there are plenty of new up-and-coming bands from California—bands such as Black Rebel Motorcycle Club, The Warlocks, and Scarling. You haven't heard of them yet but wait a few years. And even if none of these bands make it big, you can be sure that it won't be long before the next big band from California hits the music world.

For **MORE!** Go to www.cambridge.org/elt/americanmore and take a quiz on this text.

Wordlist

Unit 1

ages /ˈeɪdʒɪz/
argument /ˈɑːrgjəmənt/
to breathe /briːð/
to brighten up /ˌbraɪtən ˈʌp/
by the way /ˌbaɪ ðə ˈweɪ/
cell /sel/
cough /kɑːf/
deadly /ˈdedli/
to desert /dɪˈzɜːrt/
digital camera /ˌdɪdʒɪtəl ˈkæmrə/
drop /drɑːp/
ever /ˈevər/
fall /fɔːl/
fever /ˈfiːvər/
flu /fluː/
game console /ˈgeɪm ˌkɑːnsoʊl/
to get in touch with /ˌget ɪn ˈtʌtʃ wɪð/
global /ˈgloʊbəl/
harbor /ˈhɑːrbər/
headphones /ˈhedfoʊnz/
illness /ˈɪlnəs/
immune /ɪˈmjuːn/
to infect /ɪnˈfekt/
influenza /ˌɪnfluˈenzə/
to be into /biː ˈɪntuː/
to mind your own business /ˌmaɪnd jər oʊn ˈbɪznɪs/
MP3 player /ˌem piː ˈθriː ˌpleɪər/
outbreak /ˈaʊtbreɪk/
pain /peɪn/
palmtop /ˈpɑːmtɑːp/
pandemic /pænˈdemɪk/
possession /pəˈzeʃən/
questionnaire /ˌkwestʃəˈner/
saxophone /ˈsæksəfoʊn/
shot /ʃɑːt/
since /sɪns/
sneeze /sniːz/
soul /soʊl/
spike /spaɪk/
to spread /spred/
to be starving /ˌbiː ˈstɑːrvɪŋ/
to sulk /sʌlk/
to take something back /ˌteɪk ... ˈbæk/
tiny /ˈtaɪni/
troubled /ˈtrʌbəld/
understanding /ˌʌndərˈstændɪŋ/

Unit 2

adventure /ədˈventʃər/
afraid /əˈfreɪd/
already /ɔːlˈredi/
always /ˈɔːlweɪz/
amateur /ˈæmətər/
amazed /əˈmeɪzd/
animated cartoons /ˌænɪmeɪt̬ɪd kɑːrˈtuːnz/
archeologist /ˌɑːrkiˈɑːlədʒɪst/
article /ˈɑːrt̬ɪkəl/
blood /blʌd/
boring /ˈbɔːrɪŋ/
buzz /bʌz/
to commit /kəˈmɪt/
cover /ˈkʌvər/
crane /kreɪn/
creative /kriˈeɪt̬ɪv/
crime /kraɪm/
currency /ˈkɜːrənsi/
diet /ˈdaɪət/
dinosaur /ˈdaɪnəˌsɔːr/
director /dəˈrektər/
economy /ɪˈkɑːnəmi/
electricity /iːlekˈtrɪsət̬i/
epic /ˈepɪk/
evil /ˈiːvəl/
funny /ˈfʌni/
gun /gʌn/
horror /ˈhɔːrər/
just /dʒʌst/
kill /kɪl/
mechanic /mɪˈkænɪk/
mosquito /məˈskiːt̬oʊ/
movie /ˈmuːvi/
nightmare /ˈnaɪtmer/
poker /ˈpoʊkər/
popcorn /ˈpɑːpkɔːrn/
population /ˌpɑːpjəˈleɪʃən/
prize /praɪz/
producer /prəˈduːsər/
recent /ˈriːsənt/
resort /rɪˈzɔːrt/
responsible /rɪˈspɑːnsəbəl/
review /rɪˈvjuː/
scary /ˈskeri/
science fiction /ˌsaɪəns ˈfɪkʃən/
scientist /ˈsaɪəntɪst/
to sign /saɪn/
special effects /ˌspeʃəl ɪˈfekts/
spymaster /ˈspaɪˌmæstər/

stunt /stʌnt/
successful /səkˈsesfəl/
terror /ˈterər/
toiletries /ˈtɔɪlətriz/
twice /twaɪs/
unusual /ʌnˈjuːʒuəl/
various /ˈveriəs/
villain /ˈvɪlən/
violent /ˈvaɪələnt/
war /wɔːr/
western /ˈwestərn/
yet /jet/

Unit 3

cache /kæʃ/
to carve out /kɑːrv ˈaʊt/
century /ˈsentʃəri/
coin /kɔɪn/
compressed /kəmˈprest/
continent /ˈkɑːntənənt/
coordinates /koʊˈɔːrdənəts/
couple /ˈkʌpəl/
to discover /dɪsˈkʌvər/
earrings /ˈɪrɪŋz/
exactly /ɪgˈzæktli/
field /fiːld/
flooded /ˈflʌdɪd/
to flow /floʊ/
fresh water /ˌfreʃ ˈwɑːt̬ər/
geocaching /ˈdʒiːoʊˌkæʃɪŋ/
glacier /ˈgleɪʃər/
GPS unit /ˌdʒiː piː ˈes ˌjuːnɪt/
ground /graʊnd/
handful /ˈhændfʊl/
to hide /haɪd/
highway /ˈhaɪweɪ/
hunt /hʌnt/
hydroelectric /ˌhaɪdroʊɪˈlektrɪk/
to keep /kiːp/
landscape /ˈlændskeɪp/
leader /ˈliːdər/
mass /mæs/
to melt /melt/
moon /muːn/
mummy /ˈmʌmi/
ocean /ˈoʊʃən/
power /ˈpaʊər/
production /prəˈdʌkʃən/
proud /praʊd/
resources /ˈriːsɔːrsɪz/
to rise /raɪz/

sensation /senˈseɪʃən/
to shrink /ʃrɪŋk/
to sign up /saɪn ˈʌp/
stone /stoʊn/
thick /θɪk/
treasure /ˈtreʒər/
to turn something on /tɜːrn ... ˈɑːn/
to water /ˈwɑːt̬ər/
waterfall /ˈwɑːt̬ərˌfɔːl/
weight /weɪt/
worried /ˈwʌrid/

Unit 4

abroad /əˈbrɑːd/
ancient /ˈeɪnʃənt/
apologize /əˈpɑːlədʒaɪz/
author /ˈɑːθər/
to behave /bɪˈheɪv/
to bump into /ˌbʌmp ˈɪntuː/
character /ˈkerəktər/
to come across /ˌkʌm əˈkrɑːs/
to decide /dɪˈsaɪd/
depressed /dɪˈprest/
determined /dɪˈtɜːrmɪnd/
dirt /dɜːrt/
disappointed /ˌdɪsəˈpɔɪntɪd/
doorbell /ˈdɔːrbel/
dynamic /daɪˈnæmɪk/
event /ɪˈvent/
extract /ˈekstrækt/
to fail /ˈfeɪl/
festival /ˈfestɪvəl/
flexible /ˈfleksɪbəl/
foreign /ˈfɔːrɪn/
to give up /gɪv ˈʌp/
helpful /ˈhelpfəl/
intelligent /ɪnˈtelɪdʒənt/
to invent /ɪnˈvent/
to investigate /ɪnˈvestɪgeɪt/
to justify /ˈdʒʌstɪfaɪ/
lentil /ˈlentəl/
location /loʊˈkeɪʃən/
to look into /ˌlʊk ˈɪntuː/
lucky charm /ˌlʌki ˈtʃɑːrm/
magpie /ˈmægpaɪ/
to make up /meɪk ˈʌp/
mark /mɑːrk/
mirror /ˈmɪrər/
mixture /ˈmɪkstʃər/
multiple choice /ˌmʌltəpəl ˈtʃɔɪs/
passionate /ˈpæʃənət/

positive /'pɑːzət̬ɪv/
to postpone /poʊst'poʊn/
principal /'prɪnsəpəl/
proof /pruːf/
to put off /pʊt 'ɑːf/
rude /ruːd/
sense /sens/
similar /'sɪmələr/
story /'stɔːri/
superstition /ˌsuːpər'stɪʃən/
superstitious /ˌsuːpər'stɪʃəs/
to sweep /swiːp/
symbol /'sɪmbəl/
to take after /ˌteɪk 'æftər/
trance /træns/
to turn down /tɜːrn 'daʊn/
to turn on /tɜːrn 'ɑːn/
web /web/
whisper /'wɪspər/
wish /wɪʃ/

Unit 5

aquarium /ə'kweriəm/
assignment /ə'saɪnmənt/
atlas /'ætləs/
auditorium /ɑːdə'tɔːriəm/
to bet /bet/
bone /boʊn/
capitol /'kæpət̬əl/
concert /'kɑːnsərt/
Congress /'kɑːngres/
to defend /dɪ'fend/
to design /dɪ'zaɪn/
exhibition /ˌeksɪ'bɪʃən/
eyewitness /'aɪwɪtnəs/
farmer's market
    /'fɑːrmərz ˌmɑːrkɪt/
to fire /'faɪər/
governor /'gʌvənər/
international
    /ˌɪntər'næʃnəl/
intonation /ˌɪntə'neɪʃən/
lousy /'laʊzi/
magnifying glass
    /'mægnɪfaɪɪŋ ˌglæs/
meaning /'miːnɪŋ/
monument /'mɑːnjəmənt/
museum /mjuː'ziəm/
nurse /nɜːrs/
park /pɑːrk/
performance
    /pər'fɔːrməns/
pilot /'paɪlət/
populous /'pɑːpjələs/
programmer
    /'proʊgræmər/

protester /'proʊtestər/
rebuilt /ˌriː'bɪlt/
ruins /'ruːɪnz/
to rule /ruːl/
service /'sɜːrvɪs/
sheepdog /'ʃiːpdɑːg/
stadium /'steɪdiəm/
superstore /'suːpərˌstɔːr/
theater /'θɪət̬ər/
vibrant /'vaɪbrənt/
wood /wʊd/
wooden /'wʊdən/

Unit 6

to allow /ə'laʊ/
apartheid /ə'pɑːrteɪt/
baseball /'beɪsbɔːl/
border /'bɔːrdər/
to break out /breɪk 'aʊt/
cassette player /kə'set
    ˌpleɪər/
cocoa bean /'koʊkoʊ ˌbiːn/
competition /ˌkɑːmpə'tɪʃən/
to dye /daɪ/
electrician /iˌlek'trɪʃən/
to end up /end 'ʌp/
grizzly bear /'grɪzli ˌber/
grown-up /'groʊnˌʌp/
helmet /'helmət/
to hibernate /'haɪbərneɪt/
housework /'haʊswɜːrk/
igloo /'ɪgluː/
immigrant /'ɪmɪgrənt/
independent
    /ˌɪndə'pendənt/
insect /'ɪnsekt/
to let /let/
llama /'lɑːmə/
native speaker /ˌneɪt̬ɪv
    'spiːkər/
olive oil /ˌɑːlɪv 'ɔɪl/
peaceful /'piːsfəl/
to pronounce
    /prə'naʊns/
refugee /ˌrefjʊ'dʒiː/
rhino /'raɪnoʊ/
salary /'sæləri/
seat /siːt/
to share /ʃer/
snowmobile /'snoʊmoʊˌbiːl/
tiring /'taɪərɪŋ/
truffle /'trʌfəl/
volume /'vɑːljuːm/
war-torn /'wɔːrtɔːrn/

Unit 7

album /'ælbəm/
bamboo /bæm'buː/
binding /'baɪndɪŋ/
blues /bluːz/
career /kə'rɪr/
clarinet /ˌkler'net/
classical /'klæsɪkəl/
compilation
    /ˌkɑːmpə'leɪʃən/
complaint /kəm'pleɪnt/
country /'kʌntri/
crazy /'kreɪzi/
drummer /'drʌmər/
folk /foʊk/
heavy metal /ˌhevi 'met̬əl/
hip-hop /'hɪpˌhɑːp/
idol /'aɪdəl/
indie /'ɪndi/
jazz /dʒæz/
lonely /'loʊnli/
to be made up of /biː
    ˌmeɪd 'ʌp əv/
massive /'mæsɪv/
metallic /mə'tælɪk/
musician /mjuː'zɪʃən/
neighbor /'neɪbər/
neither /'niːðər/
noise /nɔɪz/
opening /'oʊpənɪŋ/
out of tune /ˌaʊt̬ əv 'tuːn/
punk /pʌŋk/
rap /ræp/
to remind /rɪ'maɪnd/
roof /ruːf/
to scream /skriːm/
to shoot /ʃuːt/
so /soʊ/
stage /steɪdʒ/
stuff /stʌf/
talent show /'tælənt ˌʃoʊ/
training /'treɪnɪŋ/
vocals /'voʊkəlz/

Unit 8

to affect /ə'fekt/
aftershock /'æftərˌʃɑːk/
to amuse /ə'mjuːz/
artist /'ɑːrt̬əst/
ashore /ə'ʃɔːr/
avalanche /'ævəlænʃ/
berry /'beri/
caption /'kæpʃən/
castaway /'kæstəweɪ/
catastrophe /kə'tæstrəfi/
coconut /'koʊkənʌt/
to collapse /kə'læps/
comic /'kɑːmɪk/
to control /kən'troʊl/

to crush /krʌʃ/
desert island /ˌdezərt
    'aɪlənd/
disaster /dɪ'zæstər/
dishwasher /'dɪʃˌwɑːʃər/
drought /draʊt/
dynamite /'daɪnəmaɪt/
earth /ɜːrθ/
earthquake /'ɜːrθkweɪk/
to erupt /ɪ'rʌpt/
to escape /ɪs'keɪp/
to evacuate /ɪ'vækjueɪt/
fox /fɑːks/
hurricane /'hɜːrɪkeɪn/
lava /'lɑːvə/
lightbulb /'laɪtˌbʌlb/
literature /'lɪt̬ərəˌtʃər/
local /'loʊkəl/
make-believe
    /'meɪkbɪˌliːv/
miracle /'mɪrəkəl/
mudslide /'mʌdslaɪd/
nuclear reactor /ˌnuːkliər
    ri'æktər/
package /'pækɪdʒ/
to panic /'pænɪk/
peers /pɪrz/
to protect /prə'tekt/
raft /ræft/
to reach /riːtʃ/
to run into /ˌrʌn 'ɪntə/
to rush /rʌʃ/
scale /skeɪl/
to serve /sɜːrv/
to shake /ʃeɪk/
signal flare /'sɪgnəl ˌfler/
to slide /slaɪd/
society /sə'saɪət̬i/
strength /streŋkθ/
suitcase /'suːtˌkeɪs/
survival /sər'vaɪvəl/
to survive /sər'vaɪv/
sympathy /'sɪmpəθi/
telephone /'teləfoʊn/
temple /'tempəl/
tremor /'tremər/
tsunami /tsu'nɑːmi/
volcano /vɑːl'keɪnoʊ/
warning /'wɔːrnɪŋ/
website /'websaɪt/
windshield wipers
    /'wɪndʃiːld ˌwaɪpərz/

Unit 9

to add /æd/
alibi /'æləbaɪ/
to babysit /'beɪbisɪt/
bill /bɪl/
bowl /boʊl/
built-in /ˌbɪlt'ɪn/

CD-ROM /ˌsiː ˌdiː ˈrɑːm/
to charge /tʃɑːrdʒ/
circular /ˈsɜːrkjələr/
clockwise /ˈklɑːkwaɪz/
coach /koʊtʃ/
definitely /ˈdefɪnətli/
diagonal /daɪˈægənəl/
digit /ˈdɪdʒɪt/
dilemma /dɪˈlemə/
doubt /daʊt/
to earn /ɜːrn/
flash drive /ˈflæʃ ˌdraɪv/
to fold /foʊld/
grade /greɪd/
half /hæf/
horizontal /ˌhɔːrɪˈzɑːntəl/
key /kiː/
keyboard /ˈkiː ˌbɔːrd/
LAN /læn/
to lead to /ˈliːd tə/
modem /ˈmoʊdəm/
to multiply /ˈmʌltəplaɪ/
notebook /ˈnoʊtbʊk/
opinion /əˈpɪnjən/
paper route /ˈpeɪpər ˌraʊt/
printer /ˈprɪntər/
relationship /rɪˈleɪʃənʃɪp/
repair /rɪˈper/
ridiculous /rɪˈdɪkjələs/
to seal /siːl/
speakers /ˈspiːkərz/
specialist /ˈspeʃəlɪst/
to subtract /səbˈtrækt/
total /ˈtoʊtəl/

Unit 10

balcony /ˈbælkəni/
to book /bʊk/
to buy /baɪ/
camping /ˈkæmpɪŋ/
to change /tʃeɪndʒ/
to check out /tʃek ˈaʊt/
delta /ˈdeltə/
den /den/
to dye /daɪ/
equipment /ɪˈkwɪpmənt/
to find out /faɪnd ˈaʊt/
flight /flaɪt/
ink /ɪŋk/
leopard /ˈlepərd/
to look at /ˈlʊk ət/
to make /meɪk/
must /mʌst/
opportunity /ˌɑːpərˈtuːnəti/
to paint /peɪnt/
park ranger /ˌpɑːrk ˈreɪndʒər/
to plot /ˈplɑːt/

to rent /rent/
safari /səˈfɑːri/
skill /skɪl/
spot /spɑːt/
surfing /ˈsɜːrfɪŋ/
to take /teɪk/
vacation /veɪˈkeɪʃən/
volunteer /ˌvɑːlənˈtɪr/
wetland /ˈwetlænd/
wilderness /ˈwɪldərnəs/
windsurfing /ˈwɪndsɜːrfɪŋ/

Unit 11

to admire /ədˈmaɪər/
alternative /ɔːlˈtɜːrnəţɪv/
appliance /əˈplaɪənts/
average /ˈævərɪdʒ/
blackout /ˈblækaʊt/
blank /blæŋk/
bottle /ˈbɑːţəl/
consumption /kənˈsʌmpʃən/
container /kənˈteɪnər/
council /ˈkaʊntsəl/
current /ˈkɜːrənt/
democracy /dɪˈmɑːkrəsi/
ecology /ɪˈkɑːlədʒi/
economy /ɪˈkɑːnəmi/
energy /ˈenərdʒi/
entrance /ˈentrəns/
to face /feɪs/
to found /faʊnd/
French fries /ˌfrentʃ ˈfraɪz/
gas pump /ˈgæs ˌpʌmp/
heat /hiːt/
hero /ˈhɪroʊ/
heroine /ˈheroʊɪn/
increase /ɪŋˈkriːs/
insulation /ˌɪnsəˈleɪʃən/
law /lɑː/
lawyer /ˈlɑːjər/
leaflet /ˈliːflət/
litterbug /ˈlɪţərbʌg/
march /mɑːrtʃ/
marine /məˈriːn/
to marry /ˈmeri/
to object /əbˈdʒekt/
to overcome /oʊvərˈkʌm/
parliament /ˈpɑːrləmənt/
petition /pəˈtɪʃən/
planner /ˈplænər/
plan of action /ˌplæn əv ˈækʃən/
to plant /plænt/
playing field /ˈpleɪɪŋ ˌfiːld/
poison /ˈpɔɪzən/
pond /pɑːnd/
to power /ˈpaʊər/
protest /ˈproʊtest/

to recycle /ˌriːˈsaɪkəl/
renewable energy /rɪˌnuːəbəl ˈenərdʒi/
rights /raɪts/
single mother /ˌsɪŋgəl ˈmʌðər/
slogan /ˈsloʊgən/
solar power /ˌsoʊlər ˈpaʊər/
source /sɔːrs/
to stand up for /ˌstænd ˈʌp fər/
to support /səˈpɔːrt/
tennis court /ˈtenɪs ˌkɔːrt/
tide /taɪd/
traditional /trəˈdɪʃənəl/
tunnel /ˈtʌnəl/
washing machine /ˈwɑːʃɪŋ məˌʃiːn/
wind turbine /ˈwɪnd ˌtɜːrbɪn/

Unit 12

to afford /əˈfɔːrd/
blonde /blɑːnd/
casual /ˈkæʒuəl/
charts /tʃɑːrts/
contrast /ˈkɑːntræst/
copper /ˈkɑːpər/
deal /diːl/
diverse /daɪˈvɜːrs/
elegant /ˈeləgənt/
to experience /ɪkˈspɪriəns/
film studio /ˈfɪlm ˌstuːdioʊ/
generation /ˌdʒenəˈreɪʃən/
to hand out /ˈhænd ˈaʊt/
handprint /ˈhændprɪnt/
handset /ˈhændset/
to identify /aɪˈdentɪfaɪ/
incredible /ɪnˈkredəbəl/
influential /ˌɪnfluˈenʃəl/
landfill /ˈlændfɪl/
material /məˈtɪriəl/
muscular /ˈmʌskjələr/
national park /ˌnæʃnəl ˈpɑːrk/
pipe /paɪp/
politician /ˌpɑːləˈtɪʃən/
to release /rɪˈliːs/
to reuse /ˌriːˈjuːz/
scheme /skiːm/
sophisticated /səˈfɪstɪˌkeɪţɪd/
sporty /ˈspɔːrţi/
strip /strɪp/
traffic cone /ˈtræfɪk ˌkoʊn/
up-and-coming /ˌʌp ənd ˈkʌmɪŋ/

waste /weɪst/

Pronunciation guide

Vowels

/iː/	real, screen
/ɪ/	dish, sit
/i/	funny
/e/	chess, bed
/æ/	bad, taxi
/ʌ/	must, done
/ʊ/	good, full
/uː/	choose, view
/ə/	dramatic, the
/ɑː/	stop, opera
/ɔː/	saw, daughter

Vowels + /r/

/ɜːr/	first, shirt
/ɑːr/	car
/ɔːr/	horse
/er/	their
/ʊr/	tourist
/ɪr/	ear
/ər/	teacher

Diphthongs

/eɪ/	play, train
/aɪ/	ice, night
/ɔɪ/	employer, noisy
/aʊ/	house, download
/oʊ/	no, window

Consonants

/p/	push
/b/	bank
/t/	time
/t̯/	butter
/d/	diary
/k/	carpet
/g/	big
/f/	surf
/v/	very
/θ/	thin
/ð/	that
/s/	sit
/z/	zero
/ʃ/	shine
/ʒ/	measure
/h/	hot
/w/	water
/tʃ/	chair
/dʒ/	joke
/m/	more
/n/	snow
/ŋ/	sing
/r/	ring
/l/	small
/j/	you

CAMBRIDGE UNIVERSITY PRESS
http://www.cambridge.org/elt/americanmore

HELBLING LANGUAGES
www.helblinglanguages.com

American MORE! 3 Student's Book
by Herbert Puchta & Jeff Stranks
with G. Gerngross C. Holzmann P. Lewis-Jones

3rd printing 2013

Printed in the United Kingdom by Latimer Trend

ISBN 978-0-521-17137-3   American MORE! 3 Student's Book with interactive CD-ROM
ISBN 978-0-521-17146-5   American MORE! 3 Workbook with Audio CD
ISBN 978-0-521-17147-2   American MORE! 3 Teacher's Book
ISBN 978-0-521-17149-6   American MORE! 3 Teacher's Resource Pack with Testbuilder CD-ROM/Audio CD
ISBN 978-0-521-17150-2   American MORE! 3 Class Audio CDs
ISBN 978-0-521-17153-3   American MORE! 3 Extra Practice Book
ISBN 978-0-521-17156-4   American MORE! 3 DVD (NTSC)

The authors would like to thank those people who have made significant contributions towards the final form of American MORE! INTERNATIONAL:

Oonagh Wade and Rosamund Cantalamessa for their expertise in working on the manuscripts, their useful suggestions for improvement, and the support we got from them.

Lucia Astuti and Markus Spielmann, Helbling Languages, Ron Ragsdale and James Dingle, Cambridge University Press, for their dedication to the project and innovative publishing vision.

Our designers, Amanda Hockin, Greg Sweetnam, Quantico, Craig Cornell, and Niels Gyde for their imaginative layouts and stimulating creativity. Also, our artwork assistants, Silvia Scorzoso and Francesca Gironi, for their dedicated work.

The publishers would like to thank the following for their kind permission to reproduce the following photographs and other copyright material:

Alamy p14, p23, p31 (geocaching), p33 (Tuvalu), p34, p50, p63, p65, p66 (indie), p69 (Beatles album cover), p70, p72 (bouzouki; tin whistle), p109, p113 (turbine; bike rider), p119 (Universal Studios), p123; **Associated Press** p109 (Al Gore); **Corbis** p15, p49 (Mrs. O'Leary and her cow), p66 (R&B), p69, p74 (US Air Force relief efforts; earthquake damage), p111, p123 (Red Hot Chilli Peppers); **Dreamstime** p6 (cd player; games console), p31 (canoeing; caving), p46 (museum; Yankee Stadium; concert), p50 (Julie), p53, p66, p70 (boy), p71, p74 (tsunami), p76 (tsunami), p83, p102, p114; **Dkimages** p32; **Gary Braasch** p33 (Pasterze Glacier); **Getty Images** p109 (Erin Brockovich); **Günter Gerngross**

p99; **Helbling Languages** p86 (modem; notebook; printer; USB stick); **Herbert Puchta** p113 (petrol station); **©iStockphoto.com** p6 (phone; sunglasses), p12, p26 (girl), p30, p31 (rock climbing), p34 (magpie), p46 (theatre; cinema; market), p50 (Anthony), p54, p56 (doctor; waiter; nurse), p62, p70 (girl), p71 (Steve), p76 (earthquake; avalanche; flood; drought), p86 (DVD-R/W; speakers; flat screen), p94, p95 (beach; camping; surfing), p102 (graffiti removers, girl weeding), p113 (solar cells on roof), p120; **Library of Congress** p49 (the Great Chicago Fire), p52; **Photos.com** p22 (Canadian flag), p56 (police officer), p95 (Statue of Liberty), p115 (Vancouver); **Shutterstock** p6, p13, p22, p25, p26 (boy), p31 (walking; mountain biking), p34 (lentils), p45, p46, p50 (James), p54 (igloo; snow mobile), p56, p58, p59, p62 (bilingual stop sign), p66 (rap; opera; jazz; country; rock; classical), p72, p74, p76, p82, p86, p93, p95, p102 (snowboarder), p110, p111 (Barack Obama), p113, p114 (Joshua tree; Walk of Fame), p115, p119, p122; **SuperStock** p102 (teens at construction site).

The publishers would like to thank the following illustrators:

Roberto Battestini; Moreno Chiacchiera; Michele Farella; Pierluigi Longo; Gastone Mencherini.

The publishers would like to thank the following for their assistance with commissioned photographs:

Ed-Imaging pp 4, 24, 44, 64, 84, 104, 114.

Every effort has been made to trace the owners of any copyright material in this book. If notified, the publisher will be pleased to rectify any errors or omissions.